To Charlaine Regammti
(meanany)

With friendly
and respect

[signature]

The
Italian
Experience
In Texas

Cav. Valentine J. Belfiglio

EAKIN PRESS ★ AUSTIN, TEXAS

FIRST EDITION

Dedicated to the memory of

My Grandfather, Valentino Belfiglio
(1882-1955)
who was born in
Roccamontepiano (Chieti) Abruzzi, Italy

And to the memory of

Giovanni Schiavo

TABLE OF CONTENTS

FOREWORD

"THANK GOD I'M AN ITALIAN." These words are written on a red and white placard which hangs above a piano in one of the rooms of a spacious law firm in North Dallas. The prominent attorney who placed it there does not speak the Italian language, knows little about Italian culture, and possesses an Anglo-American surname. His father was born in Italy, but his mother was of Irish descent. What factors account for the Italian identity of this man? *The Italian Experience in Texas* provides insightful answers to intriguing questions such as this one.

This important book tells the story of the Italian presence in Texas from earliest to modern times. It is a rich and brilliant chronicle of cultural assimilation and retention and the tragiocomedy of ethnic experiences. In the humorous, dire, joyous, and sorrowful accounts of Italian immigrants one sees all humankind, just as in the history, folklore, growth and decay of the Italian communities in Texas one sees the experiences of all immigrant cultures. Italian miners and railroad workers, Italian farmers and artists — the variety of life, the endlessness of assimilation, the search for community and identity — these, the universal themes, dominate the book. Whether he is describing the Texas War of Independence, the drudgery of everyday living, or the struggle for upward social mobility, Cavaliere Valentino Belfiglio always writes with the simplicity, ease, and purity that are the mark of an expert. Inventive, amusing, magnetic, sad, alive with unforgettable men and women, and with a truth and understanding that strike the soul, *The Italian Experience in Texas* is an extremely valuable contribution to the art of nonfiction.

Giovanni E. Schiavo
Plano, Texas
December 19, 1982

v

CHARLES A. SIRINGO
— *Courtesy Siringo, Chas. A.; A Texas Cowboy.*
Chicago, M. Umbenstock & Co., 1885

PREFACE

In 1885, after fifteen years with the trail herds, a Texas cowboy published a fascinating account of his life on the range. His book, titled *A Texas Cowboy,* is a classic. It is written in an interesting, descriptive style. There are chapters on cow punching, roping steers, buying cattle, and the author's experience living among Indians. Frank Dobie states that the writer "was not only the first authentic cowboy to publish an autobiography; of all cowboys, both spurious and authentic, who have recollected in print he was the most prolific in autobiographic variations. No record of cowboy life has supplanted his rollicky, reckless, realistic chronicle." [1]

The author of *A Texas Cowboy* was Angelo "Charlie" Siringo, the son of an Italian immigrant. He was born in Matagorda County, Texas, on February 7, 1855. John Hays Hammond described him as "a slender, wiry man, dark-eyed, dark-moustached, modest . . . interesting, resourceful, courageous." Siringo published six more books before his death in 1928. But he was not the only Italian cowboy to ride the Texas plains. [2]

Italian-born Don Louis Cardis was a native of Piedmont and served as a captain in Garibaldi's army before migrating to the United States in 1854. Ten years later he came to El Paso, learned to speak fluent Spanish, and won the confidence of the Spanish-speaking citizens. He operated the stage line to Fort Davis and quietly used his spare time building a political power base. Cardis was

[1] Charles A. Siringo, *A Texas Cowboy.* (New York: William Sloane, 1950), p. x. With an introduction by J. Frank Dobie.
[2] *Ibid.,* p. xxxiv.

described as a delicately featured individual with a black moustache and chin whiskers. He appeared in public wearing a Prince Albert coat, immaculate white linen shirt, and black bow tie. Because he was only a fair public speaker, Cardis preferred to work behind the scenes. His friends considered him persuasive, witty, intelligent, and suave. Beginning in 1874, he served two terms in the Texas State Legislature, where one of his colleagues was another Italian Texan named Decimus et Ultimus Barziza.[3]

Many people, including native Texans, are not aware of the Italian presence in Texas during the nineteenth century. Yet Italians have been part of the history of the state since 1540. Until now, the Italian experience in Texas has not been recorded in book form. You are about to read previously unwritten pages of Texas history.

[3] Anne Hammon, West Texas and the State Constitutional Convention of 1875. M.A. Thesis. Texas Technological College, Lubbock, Texas, 1935, pp. 20-32.

The
Italian
Experience
In Texas

WHY ITALIANS CAME
TO TEXAS (1870-1914)

*Haud facile emergunt quorum virtutibus
obstat/res angusta domi.*

*Men do not easily succeed who are held
back by straitened circumstances at home.*
— Juvenal III, 164.

In 1900 Enrico Cerrachio crossed the Atlantic Ocean
by steamship. The Italian sculptor ate little on the voyage from Italy to America. He was so overjoyed at the
sight of the New York skyline that he threw his tools
overboard, believing that he could easily purchase better
ones. Cerrachio soon became disillusioned. He spoke no
English, possessed little money, and people generally
were not impressed with his credentials. For a time Cerrachio slept on a park bench and ate at a Bowery soup
kitchen. In desperation he joined a work gang clearing
land for a railroad, but eventually he was able to resume
sculpting. The Italian settled in Houston and became a
naturalized American citizen in 1905. Before his death in
1956 he had made a significant impact on Texas art.[1]

Italians came to Texas for many reasons, but some
general trends are discernible. During the seventeenth,
eighteenth, and first half of the nineteenth centuries, the
relatively few Italians who journeyed to Texas were
mostly explorers, adventurers, or missionaries. But from

---

[1] Frances Battaile Fisk, *A History of Texas Artists and Sculptors.*
(Abilene: Fisk, 1928), pp. 216-218; Esse Forrester-O'Brien, *Art and
Artists of Texas.* (Dallas: Tardy, 1935), p. 246.

the time of Italian unification (1861) until World War I, Italian emigration can be divided into two periods distinguished according to the number of emigrants, their place of origin and destination, and the amount of government regulation.

EMIGRATION FROM NORTHERN ITALY

The first period, from unification to the end of the nineteenth century, was characterized by a fairly heavy outpouring of emigrants from *Alta Italia* (the northern regions). Nearly two-thirds of the Italian emigrants of this period hailed from the North. Some of these people were urban day laborers. The prosperous countries of Europe, such as Germany, Switzerland, and France were their favored destinations. However, Northern Italians also went to America and a number of them settled in Texas. Most of the early emigrants sought personal fortunes and were determined to return eventually to their homelands. At this time the Italian government offered little protection or advice to the would-be emigrant. Few restrictions were placed on emigration, although officials in Rome tended to view the practice with displeasure.[2]

Northern Italian *contadini* (peasant farmers) emigrated from those mountainous areas of Lombardy, Piedmont, and Venetia, where the soil was relatively unproductive. The ordinary small estates in these localities, with their short growing season and stony soil, could not yield the *contadini* enough productivity for even moderately comfortable standards of living. Their lack of agricultural knowledge, crude farm implements, and a heavy land tax seriously eroded profit margins. In 1905 the average daily wage of the *contadini* of northern Italy was thirty-six cents, compared to thirty-four cents per day in southern Italy.[3] Between May 30 and August

---

[2] Herbert J. Gans, "Some Comments on the History of Italian Migration and the Nature of Historical Research," *International Migration Review.* Vol. I New Sources (Summer, 1967), pp. 71-72.

[3] Dati Statistici sul Mercato del Lavoro in Agricoltura nel 1905, **Roma**, 1905, p. 146.

18, 1907, representatives of the U.S. Immigration Commission made a tour of Italy in order to prepare a report on the socio-economic conditions in that country. They discovered that in spite of higher wages in America, ". . . there is but little difference in the cost of food in the United States and Italy, but there is a wide difference in the standard of living in the two countries." [4]

While visiting Lombardy, the Immigration Commission observed that a large part of the land of that region was owned by wealthy proprietors, who leased it in large and small parcels. "Some of the tenants in turn sublet to small farmers. The farm buildings generally belong either to the owner of the land or to groups of lessees who have been in the business so long that they have established a practically permanent control of the land they occupy. The small farmer leasing the land from one of the two classes above him pays rent for the buildings, the average rent of farmhouses being about six dollars per year per room. There is no fixed rule governing the terms of contracts for lands, but most of the farmers pay at least a portion of their rent in produce, and it is said that comparatively few pay entirely in cash. The Commission was informed that the value of the land, generally speaking, was from $250 to $300 per acre, with a tendency to increase. Few of the small farmers handle much money during the year. They are compelled to lead an exceedingly frugal life, accumulating just enough produce in the summer to carry them and their families through the winter." [5]

Conditions for the industrial workers of northern Italy were somewhat better than those of their agricultural counterparts. Miners and diggers earned an average daily wage of fifty-eight cents in 1903, and seventy cents in 1907. But all things considered, the higher

[4] Emigration Conditions in Europe: Italy. Reports of the Immigration Commission, Vol. 12 (Senate Document No. 748, 61st Cong., 3rd. sess., 1911), pp. 163-164.

[5] *Ibid.,* p. 155.

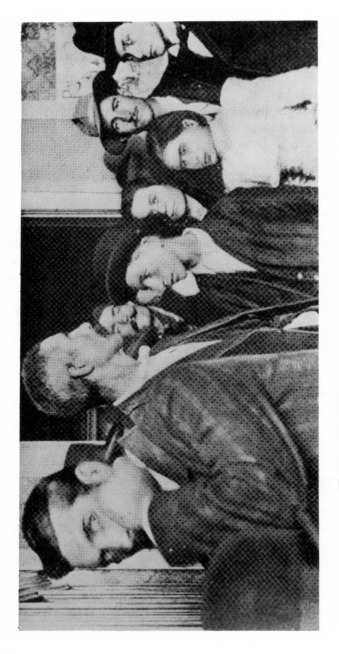

ITALIAN EMIGRANTS departure from Gualtieri.
— *Courtesy Brandenburg, Broughton. Imported Americans,
New York, Frederick A. Stokes Co., 1904*

industrial wages merely compensated for the higher cost of living in the industrial communities. According to the U.S. Immigration Commission: "Certainly the wages paid, and the opportunity to work afforded to skilled laborers is not sufficiently high to prevent the emigration of this class, for from July 1, 1898, to June 30, 1909, 56,854, or 16.6 per cent, of all North Italians, and 199,024, or 11.6 per cent, of all South Italians, admitted to the United States were classed as skilled." [6] The low wages paid to the *contadini* and *braccianti* (day laborers) of *Alta Italia,* caused many of these people to emigrate to foreign lands in search of better lifestyles. Tradesmen and laborers who could not rise above the poverty level of the other people of their locality were also encouraged to emigrate.[7]

EMIGRATION FROM SOUTHERN ITALY

The second period of Italian emigration occurred from about 1880 to the outbreak of World War I. It was primarily an emigration from the *Mezzogiorno* (the regions of southern Italy) and oriented toward North and South America. The Italian Emigration Law of January 31, 1901, attempted to protect those who chose to leave by managing the different stages of their emigration process. The law prescribed only four ports of emigration: Naples, Genoa, Palermo, and Messina.[8] Operating through local committees the General Commissariat of Emigration regulated the recruitment of labor and aided emigrants from the time of their departure to their arrival in host countries. Officials in Rome also spoke out against what they considered to be unfair recruitment

[6] *Ibid.,* p. 173.

[7] Robert F. Foerster, *The Italian Emigration of Our Times.* (London: Cambridge, 1924), pp. 106-126.

[8] For further discussion of the Italian system of regulating the carriage of steerage passengers at sea, consult: Šteerage Legislation, 1819-1908, Reports of the Immigration Commission, Vol. 39 (Senate Document No. 758, 61st Cong., 3rd sess., 1911).

practices. In 1904, Cav. Egisto Rossi, Royal Italian Commissioner of Emigration denounced ". . . the agents of certain steamship lines, whose only interest was the sale of steamship tickets on the largest possible scale." [9] On March, 15, 1908, the Commissioner of Emigration issued a circular designed to discourage emigration under labor contracts to certain ports in the United States. The circular declared that:

> The royal consular authorities for the States of Mississippi, Louisiana, Arkansas, Florida, Alabama, and Texas . . . have reported upon the deplorable conditions under which many of our compatriots exist who have emigrated . . . in conformity with contract-labor agreements, . . . Chief among the illegal practices . . . is that of propragating false information, describing in glowing terms . . . the high wages paid.[10]

A major reason why Italian officials attempted to discourage emigration was that many of the best Italian laborers were leaving the country. It was mostly young men with initiative, purpose, and energy who dared to venture abroad to seek their fortunes. The elderly, the destitute, the faint-hearted or slothful, and the feeble, usually remained behind. The peak year for Italian emigration was 1913, when 872,598 people left the country.[11] But the economic woes of southern Italy began much earlier.

With the population of Italy increasing rapidly after 1871, the country became overpopulated. At the turn of the century, economic conditions in the south were far worse than in the north. Professor Francesco Nitti wrote in 1907 that: ". . . northern Italy has thirty-six percent of

---

[9] "Italy Wants Her Sons To Stay At Home," *New York Times.* Vol. LIII, No. 16,907, March 12, 1904, p. 6.

[10] Government of Italy, Department of Foreign Affairs, Circular in Re-Emigration To The United States, Circular No. 17, Commissioner of Emigration, Rome, March 15, 1908, pp. 1-2.

[11] Gans, "Some Comments on the History of Italian Migration and the Nature of Historical Research," *op. cit.,* pp. 71-72.

the population, forty-seven percent of the total wealth, and about sixty percent of the national savings, while southern Italy, exclusive of Sicily and Sardinia, has twenty-six percent of the population, 20.6 percent of the wealth, and only 10.3 percent of the savings." [12] In the *Mezzogiorno* there were few modern public works, little industry, banditry was common, and less than ten percent of the adult males were able to read and write.[13] The Italian class system was rigid, and sons rarely deviated from the professions of their fathers. In addition, widespread stripping of forests during the eighteenth and nineteenth centuries caused changes in the flow of streams, soil erosion, a predisposition to land slides, and a lowering of the humidity in many places. All of these factors adversely affected the cultivation of crops. To make matters worse, outbreaks of malaria and cholera became more common, and a series of earthquakes devastated parts of Calabria, Basilicata, and Sicily between 1905 and 1908.

Because of these factors Italy produced insufficient food to meet the needs of all of its people. Also, the country lacked several important natural resources, and the Italian government failed to facilitate an equitable distribution of the resources that were available. Instead, Rome imposed the legal system of the more industrialized Piedmont upon the agricultural *Mezzogiorno*. The result was that the southern *contadini* were required to send taxes north. In fact, the tax on Sicilians rose thirty percent over the rate imposed by the Bourbons.[14] Unfortunately, most of the fertile land of southern Italy was owned by the nobility, professional groups, and the clergy. Piedmontese politicians, bureaucrats, church offi-

[12] Francesco S. Nitti, *La ricchezza dell' Italia.* (Napoli, 1904), p. 120.

[13] J. R. Commons, *Races and Immigrants in America.* New York, 1907, p. 72.

[14] Members of the French family of Bourbon who founded dynasties in France, Spain, and Naples (Charles III).

cials, and the *latifondisti* (owners of large landed estates) evaded the burden of taxation, and the taxes fell squarely upon the *contadini*. The predicament of the peasants worsened. In 1910 the Italian Parliament reported that a few hundred *latifondisti* owned or controlled the major part of the *Mezzogiorno*.[15]

The poor agricultural system prevalent in the southern part of Italy aggravated the economic situation there. Obsolete methods of cultivation, and conditions of land ownership and administration were counterproductive to economic growth. The average holding of independent *contadini* became even of smaller acreage through the custom of *frazionamento,* dividing the property among the sons upon the death of the father. The great landowners, as they controlled more land and power, moved into larger cities, leaving the management of their estates to *gabelloti* (landleasers). Owner neglect, contracts *(mezzadria)* which encouraged exploitation of the soil, and a failure to use profits to improve the land were commonplace.[16] General productivity was low and as a result, the *giornalieri* (day laborers) suffered great economic hardships.

The Italian peasants did not always accept their unfair status passively. Organized revolts in Naples and Sicily challenged the government tax collectors in 1862 and 1863, respectively. But battalions of *Bersaglieri* (colorful, special corps of light infantry) assaulted the insurgents, and the oppressive tax policy continued. A tax on mules forced the sale of many plow mules, and the reintroduction of a heavy grist tax on grain in 1868 forced most farmers to sell substantial portions of the grain they produced. This sharply reduced the amount of food available to the *contadini*. Then in the 1880s, the French government imposed a heavy tariff against Italian

[15] Emigration. (Facts About Italy Series, No. 27). New York: Istituto Italiano di Cultura, May 1972), pp. 18-19.

[16] Jan Brogger, *Montevarse: A Study of Peasant Society and Culture in Southern Italy.* (Bergen: Universitetsforlaget, 1971), pp. 21-52.

wines. This tariff seriously hurt the wine-making industries of Calabria, Apulia, and Sicily. The citrus fruit industries of Basilicata, Calabria, and Sicily also suffered as Florida and California developed their own groves and American imports of Italian oranges and lemons fell sharply in the following decades.[17]

The living and working conditions of many southern Italian peasants in 1907 were deplorable. The U.S. Immigration Commission observed that ". . . in most sections of Italy . . . every available bit of ground was utilized, . . . there was not a single plow throughout the whole of one province visited, the ground being broken by hand implements and cultivated in the same way. The grain was reaped with a sickle and there were no modern farming machinery of any character . . . in southern Italy, the people practically all live in villages and many go several miles to and from their work daily, sometimes in carts carrying fifteen to twenty workers, including men and women and children of both sexes . . . women . . . carry burdens up to two hundreds pounds on their heads."[18] The *contadini* lived in huts which were mostly low, one-room hovels, often with no opening except for the door. The floor was of earth or sometimes of stone. The furniture was usually one or two beds, and a bench or wooden chest, or perhaps a chair, and fires were built on a stone hearth. The diet of the Italian peasantry consisted of potatoes, beans, *pasta*, soup, wine, *polenta* (a cornmeal dish), and bread. Even in plentiful times meat was ordinarily eaten only once a week. It is not difficult to understand why farmers from Basilicata, Campania, Sicily, and other southern regions decided to emigrate to North Africa, South America, and the United States.[19] Many young men also desired to leave Italy to escape military conscription and parental domination.

[17] Anna Maria Ratti, "Italian Migration Movements, 1876 to 1926," in National Bureau of Economic Research, *International Migrations*. II. New York, 1929-31.

[18] Senate Document No. 748, *op. cit.*, p. 154.

[19] Foerster, *The Italian Emigration of Our Times, op. cit.*, pp. 83-105.

THE LURE OF TEXAS

In contrast to the harsh economic conditions of the *Mezzogiorno,* and *Alta Italia* lay the sparsely settled, unclaimed distant American West, of which Texas was the largest state. Whereas in Italy land was scarce and men were many, in Texas there was much land and few men. The last quarter of the nineteenth century brought not only the close of the frontier and a cattle boom to Texas but also remarkable economic growth, especially in commerce and industry. During this period the population of the state tripled, and men mined coal at Thurber and constructed an extensive network of railroad lines. Because of generous purchase terms offered by the state, owners operated most West Texas farms. Many of these people came from the numerous tenant farms in the eastern part of Texas.

Between 1821 and 1836 an estimated 38,000 settlers, on promises of 4,000 acres per family for small fees, trekked from the United States into the Texas territory. In the thirty years before the Civil War came shiploads of Germans, Poles, Czechs, Swedes, Norwegians, Irish, and a few Italians, who suffered many hardships while they established homes and farms in the frontier land. By 1850, approximately 33,000 Germans, one-fifth of the state's population, had settled there. It was difficult to acquire land in Europe, and the opportunity to obtain large quantities of it in Texas was an impelling motive for many immigrants.[20] In the early years of statehood, Texas officials established the precedent of using their vast public domain for public benefit. At first, they sold or traded the land to eliminate the huge debt remaining from the war of independence and early years of the Republic. The state had paid all of its debts by 1855 and still had over ninety-eight million acres of open domain. Texas authorities gave away land for internal improvements, veterans grants, capital construction, and the

[20] L. J. Wortham, *History of Texas.* Vol. II, pp. 182-194.

ITALIAN IMMIGRANTS preparing to serve a meal on the *Lahn* from the foodtanks and bread baskets.
— *Courtesy Brandenburg, Broughton. Imported Americans New York, Frederick A. Stokes Co., 1904*

settlement of boundary disputes. More than thirty-two million acres were donated to promote railroad construction. During the post-Civil War years numerous families from war-ravaged southern plantations moved to farms and ranches in the Southwest. Communities of farming families of Swedish, Polish, and Irish backgrounds, who were living in the North Central states, came to Texas seeking relief from the tight economy.

Meanwhile, other settlers arrived from Europe, including Belgians, Danes, and Greeks. Many of these people moved to the cities and became craftsmen and shopkeepers. During 1876 more than 400,000 people came to Texas, and by 1877 they had secured almost five million acres of land.[21] The total foreign-born white population of Texas in 1900 was 179,357, and this represented 7.5 percent of the white population. By 1920 the number had increased to 360,519 (9.5%). At that time 69.2 percent of the foreign-born residents were Mexicans, 8.6 percent were Germans, 3.6 percent were Czechs, and 2.2 percent were Italians.[22]

During the late 1870s, the Italian immigration to Texas had begun to substantially increase. Italians settled in the lower Brazos Valley, in Montague County, and on the Galveston County mainland. They also worked the rich coal mines at Thurber, and helped to construct a railroad between Victoria and Rosenberg. Major urban settlements developed in Houston, Galveston, and San Antonio. Many Italians were weary of farming, and chose instead to work in construction, mining, or other areas. They came to the state for the same reasons that led them to other lands: but primarily to obtain their own farms and/or to better their fortunes. People who had been unable to prosper in Italy came seeking a new start. Young men who sought greater opportunities

[21] Ralph W. Steen, *History of Texas.* (Austin: The Steck Company, 1939), p. 367.

[22] United States Census Reports, Volume I (Twelfth Census); Abstract of the Fourteenth Census of the United States.

than their home communities offered came to thrive with the state. Persons in search of adventure hoped to find it in Texas, and in many instances their wishes were amply fulfilled.

Research by Josef J. Barton (1975) indicates that in all voluntary immigrant movements, the few precede the many, and solitary individuals lead the few. Barton conducted extensive studies of Italians, Rumanians, and Slovaks in Cleveland, Ohio. He discovered that where there are no hindrances to movement, migration proceeds according to a regular sequence of stages. "In the earliest stage, the pioneer emigrant, motivated largely by private aspirations for a better life, journeys alone to a new society in search of a new position. A successful pioneer may communicate with family and friends at home and persuade them to follow him. The second stage is the development of a minor stream of migrants from one particular place to another. If this intermediate stage establishes a settlement, then a mass migration follows as villagers are carried forward by a pervasive social momentum. This third stage typically produces large urban settlements where immigrants form ethnic groups by establishing societies, parishes, and newspapers." [23]

Italian immigration patterns in Texas support Barton's contentions. In the earliest stage, men such as Antonio Saladino for the Brazos Valley Italians, and Antonio Bruni for San Antonio were the first catalysts of the Italian immigrations to Texas. A few men provided the initial direction or focus of the immigration. Even from the beginning, the earliest Italian pioneers acted upon the advice of persons whom they trusted. Later, railroad and steamship advertisements, and notices published in the Italian language supplemented letters and word-of-mouth information.[24] Several places in Texas ex-

[23] Josef J. Barton, *Peasants and Strangers: Italians, Rumanians, and Slovaks in an American City: 1890-1950.* (Cambridge: Harvard University Press, 1975), p. 33.

[24] U.S. Congress, House of Representatives, Report of Consul-General Edmond Jussen, Vienna, July 24, 1888, Misc. Doc. 572, pt. 2,

perienced the development of a minor stream of migrants from one place to another. Examples are Bryan, San Antonio, Galveston, Houston, Thurber, and Montague County. Some of these people formed urban settlements where the immigrants formed ethnic groups by establishing societies, parishes, and newspapers. Examples are Galveston, Houston, and San Antonio.

Most of the immigrants coming to America landed at ports on the eastern seaboard — New York, Baltimore, Boston, and Philadelphia — the focal points of transatlantic shipping. A majority of the immigrant-carrying steamship companies sailed to them. Consequently, these ports became great centers of immigration. Texas ports lay outside the major world trade routes. Yet, even in the 1850s, emigrant-carrying sailing vessels made regular trips from North German ports to Galveston. Many Italian immigrants who eventually settled in Texas traveled overland and boarded ships at either Palermo or Genoa. Citizenship records indicate that most Sicilians arrived in Texas through Galveston from New Orleans, and that most Piedmontese, Venetians, and other northern Italians arrived in New York and later migrated to Texas after sojourns in other states. The Lombards brought directly to Texas by Count Giuseppe Telfener in 1881 for the purpose of railroad construction were an exception to this rule.

Settlement patterns and information taken from declarations of intention to become citizens indicate that virtually all of the Italian immigrants were farmers, miners, or unskilled laborers.[25] They ranged from infants to elderly men and women, but a majority of the earliest migrants were males between the ages of fourteen and

50th Cong., 1st sess., 1889, Reports of Diplomatic and Consular Officers Concerning Emigration from Europe to the United States, 97-98.

[25] U.S. Congress, Senate. Reports of the Immigration Commission, Statistical Review of Immigration 1820-1910. Distribution of Immigrants 1850-1900. Sen. Doc. 756, 61st Cong., 3rd sess., 1911, p. 339.

forty-four.[26] The initial settlement pattern of the Sicilians of the Brazos Valley snaked along the river, and then fanned into the surrounding communities. A large number of them moved to the Galveston County mainland after the flood of 1899. Italians in other areas spread from the mother colonies into surrounding areas, and moved to urban centers in Galveston, Houston, San Antonio, Dallas, and other parts of the country. However, most of the Italians living in Thurber and Victoria County returned to Italy or moved to other parts of the United States when their services were no longer needed in the coal mines or in railroad construction.

No specialized studies have been conducted about the Italian who returned to Modena, Venice, and Piedmont, after the Thurber mines closed in 1921, or the Lombards who returned to the vicinity of Como after the rail line between Victoria and Rosenberg was completed in 1882. Oil strikes in the nearby Ranger field caused the closing of the Thurber mines, and construction on extensions of the railroad line was halted after Texas repealed all land grants to railroad builders. Therefore, the immediate reason why many of these Italians left Texas was a lack of employment, and this experience could have been traumatic for some of them. According to a classification scheme developed by Francesco Cerase (1974), this type of return would be called a "return of failure." Cerase's generalized studies indicate that "What remains of their experience in the new society is a sense of suffering, fear, and abandonment, mixed with the memory of 'marvels,' incomprehensible 'great things,' seen through amazed eyes." [27]

But there were positive aspects of return migrations to Italy. The report of the U.S. Immigration Commission (1911), indicates that returned migrants with their sav-

[26] Senate Documents No. 748, *op. cit.,* p. 178.

[27] Francesco P. Cerase, "Expectations and Reality: A Case of Return Migration From the United States to Southern Italy," *International Migration Review.* Vol. 8, No. 26, Summer 1974, p. 249.

ings provided one of the main resources for the life of their villages. In addition, these *americani* (return Italian migrants) tended to be cleaner, neater, and better dressed than other peasants of the village. A majority of their homes were built or remodeled with numerous modern comforts. In addition, they had been imbued with democratic ideals and "were no longer ready to address those in higher social positions with great deference. Moreover, the returned emigrants as a body are much more progressive than their old neighbors who have remained at home, and generally their standard of living is much higher ... the returned emigrants have pointed the way to better things than the Italian peasant is accustomed to and has demonstrated that they are attainable." [28]

THE ITALIAN COMMUNITIES IN TEXAS

For those Italians who chose to remain in Texas, the expansion of their settlements proceeded slowly. Those who moved to new locations were seldom out of touch with friends and relatives living in the older settlements. Seasoned immigrants led the way. The groups that established new communities were usually composed of extended families, or several families that had lived as neighbors in Texas. Once these pioneers established a new community, others might follow. In order to survive and prosper economically, Italian Texans learned to grow cotton and corn on Texas soil, to speak the English language, and to adapt to their new environment. They purchased land, opened businesses, and acquired a degree of geographic mobility. Italian immigrants arrived in Texas not as alienated and passive peoples, but as active members of coherent societies. They attempted to recreate communities that met their needs as individuals and as members of a group. The recreation was the ethnic community. The pillars supporting that community

[28] Senate Document No. 748, *op. cit.*, pp. 231-232.

were the immigrant church, the Italian language press, and the benevolent-fraternal organizations. Each of these pillars had its origins in Europe. Yet each was formed and underwent continuous transition to meet the changing needs of the membership of the ethnic community in Texas.

Most Italian settlements in Texas established an immigrant church: such as the St. Anthony Catholic Church built in Bryan in 1896, and the San Francesco Di Paola Catholic Church built in San Antonio in 1927. Italians also supported an Italian language press in major Texas cities. The first Italian language newspaper, *Il Messaggiero Italiano,* was published in Galveston in 1906, and others were published in San Antonio, Houston, and Dallas in subsequent years. Several benevolent-fraternal associations also existed in Texas. Studies by John W. Briggs (1978) of the Italian communities in Rochester, New York; Utica, New York; and Kansas City, Missouri; reveal that the immigrants patterned societies in America on their associational activities in southern Italy.[29] The author of this work discovered through taped interviews that many Italian immigrants in Texas also belonged to *Mezzogiorno* societies, and that when they arrived in the state they established organizations that paralleled southern Italian institutions in structure and function.[30] Examples are the *Societa Italiana de Mutuo Soccorso* founded in San Antonio in 1880, and the *Societa di Colonizzazione Italiana del Texas,* founded in Bryan about 1888. These societies offered services similar to the associational societies of the villages from which these people came — in the areas of health, life, and unemployment insurance; popular education; producer and consumer cooperatives; and fellowship.

The labor-union experience gained in Italy by some

[29] John W. Briggs, *An Italian Passage: Immigrants To Three American Cities, 1890-1930.* (New Haven: Yale University Press, 1978), pp. 260-278.

[30] *Italia Annuario Statistico,* 1905-1907, Roma, p. 14.

northern Italians, such as Lorenzo Santi of Modena, gave them the necessary experience to play leading roles in the local chapter of the United Mine Workers of America at Thurber, Texas. According to the *Annuario Statistico* for 1905-1907, there were 2,950 industrial unions in Italy in 1907, with a total of 362,533 members. Between 1901 and 1904 there were 3,032 industrial strikes, involving 621,737 workers, and from sixty-three to eighty percent of the strikes were reported as "successful," or "partly successful." [31] The Italian ethnic group in Texas served as a means of self-identification; it provided a network of organizations that allowed the immigrants to confine their intimate, personal relationships to the Italian community. Renewed immigration, increased population density, the rise of a second generation of prosperous farmers, businessmen, and community leaders, all promoted a climate conducive to the development of ethnic organizations. For example, the Christopher Columbus Italian Society of San Antonio was founded in 1890 by Carlo Solaro and twenty-eight other Italians. This organization is still in existence today. But some Italians desired a broader definition of their identity and as a consequence joined national Italian organizations such as Unico National, and the Order of the Sons of Italy. The affiliation with the national societies was part of the maturation process, a training ground for the future leaders of current Texas-based ethnic organizations, such as the American Italian Association of El Paso, the Italian Club of Dallas, and the Federation of American Italian Clubs of Greater Houston.

ITALIAN TEXANS TODAY

The early Italian communities in Texas allowed the Italians living within them to gradually integrate into the broader culture and society. That is, these communities brought Italians into contact with the dominant,

[31] *Ibid.,* p. 18.

southern Anglo-American culture, while providing them with sufficient support to confront their new environment with less cultural and economic trauma than they would have experienced by attempting to immediately blend into the cultural mainstream. The benevolent-fraternal associations played an important part in the ethnic community's development and was part and parcel of the assimilation process. Italian Texans have been largely assimilated into the local culture. Most of the traditional attitudes and recreational activities of the *contadini* of the *Mezzogiorno* are no longer held or practiced today by the Italian Americans living in Bryan, Dickinson, and other parts of the state. Feelings concerning *campanilismo* (localism), the distrust of outsiders, a negative attitude towards education, and political apathy have largely disappeared. Football has replaced soccer as a favorite spectator sport of modern Italian Texans, and younger members of the group dance to the rhythm of contemporary American music, rather than to the *tarantella* and other traditional Italian dances. *Cerimonialità* (ceremonialism), which was primarily perpetuated by the women of the community at weddings, funerals, and holidays, has evolved into novel forms, which have little similarities to traditional forms.

In spite of the assimilation process, Italian Texans still retain a measure of distinctiveness today. The clues for this lie in their retention of certain distinguishing cultural traits. Given the possession of an Italian surname or maiden name, *italianità* (Italianism) often varies with the following factors: membership in the Roman Catholic Church, pride in the achievements of Italy in the fields of music and art, knowledge of Italian terms and phrases, knowledge of customs pertaining to the preparation, cooking, and eating of Italian cuisine, and familiarity with Italian games, dances, and other forms of recreation. In addition, attachment to family life, *cor-*

tesia[32] (politeness, obligingness), and devotion to the *vicinato* (neighborhood) remain strong among most third-generation Italians living in Texas. Most of these people are still primarily concerned with local political, economic, and social issues. Although a few of them have held local political offices, and seats in the Texas State House of Representatives, none have been elected to national office.

In 1981, the author interviewed 224 married, third-generation Italian Texans living in small towns and rural areas in order to determine their ethnic attitudes. He discovered that 64 percent (143) of them had spouses with Italian surnames or maiden names. Of the remainder, 26 percent (58) had married Irish or German Catholics, and 10 percent (23) were married to persons who did not fall into one of these three categories. The interviews indicate that an "Italian consciousness" does not exclusively depend upon the choice of a marriage partner, language, religion, or any other factor or combination of factors. These matters merely contribute or detract from the formation and maintenance of an ethnic identity. What is essential to the existence of *italianità* is a group perception of having accomplished important things in the past, and the desire to accomplish them in the future. However, it is interesting to note in passing that visits to Italy by married couples who are both of Italian lineage, and people of Italian descent who study the Italian language often experience a revitalization of their identity as Italians.

Ethnic identity among Italian Texans depends upon common values and sympathies. It exists whenever people share a common outlook and agree that they are a distinct group who ought to associate with one another. Italian Texans living in small towns and rural areas today still form clubs based on an ethnic identification as Italian. These groups host festivals, dinners, *bocce* tour-

---

[32] *Cortesia* — refers to a very elaborate ritual of how one must conduct oneself towards the family, friends, guests, and society at large.

naments,[33] family reunions, and mutual aid programs. They also participate in church activities and civic events. Annual Columbus Day celebrations continue to be a part of the festive life of these communities. Thus, Italians have adapted to their new environment by adopting traits of the dominant culture. However, third-generation Italian Texans have not become totally assimilated, in that they have retained a sense of group identity. Most of these people are proud of their ancestry. They are also proud of their contributions toward making Texas a better place in which to live.

It is an interesting historical fact that when the first Anglo-American settlements established themselves between the Brazos and Colorado rivers around 1823, they were latecomers to Texas by comparison, as the Italian and Spanish had been exploring the territory for almost 200 years!

TABLE I. Foreign-Born Italians Resident in Texas: 1870-1920.

Year	Number of Italians
1870	186
1880	539
1890	2,107
1900	3,942
1910	7,190
1920	8,024

Sources: Compendium of the Ninth Census of the United States (Washington, 1872), 392-393.

Compendium of the Tenth Census of the United States (Washington, 1883), Part I, 486-87.

Abstract of the Eleventh Census of the United States (Washington, 1894), 38-39.

United States Census Reports, Volume I (Twelfth Census) (Washington, 1901), clxxiv.

---

[33] *Bocce* — a game somewhat resembling bowls.

Abstract of the Thirteenth Census of the United States (Washington, 1914), 204-207.

Abstract of the Fourteenth Census of the United States (Washington, 1920), 308-309.

TABLE II. Italian Population of Five Selected Texas Counties: 1900.

County	Number of Italians
Galveston	560
Brazos	553
Erath	429
Harris	392
Bexar	316
Others	1,692
Total	3,942

Source: United States Census Office, Twelfth Census of the United States, 1900, Population, Part I, Washington, D.C., 1901, pp. 783-786.

TABLE III. Number of Italians Going to Texas, Fiscal Years 1899 to 1910.

Year	Northern Italians*	Southern Italians
1899	114	96
1900	121	69
1901	130	111
1902	230	121
1903	227	151
1904	170	238
1905	183	239
1906	221	229
1907	287	284
1908	151	216
1909	176	122
1910	105	202
Total	2,115	2,078

Source: U.S., Congress, Senate. *Reports of the Immigration Commission. Statistical Review of Immigration 1820-1910. Distribution of Immigrants 1850-1900.* Sen. Doc. 756, 61st Cong., 3rd sess., 1911, p. 339.

* The Bureau of Immigration of 1911 followed the general practice of ethnologists of that time by dividing the people of Italy into two groups — North Italians and South Italians. The former were natives of the regions of Piedmont, Lombardy, Venetia, and Emilia, and the latter natives of the remainder of continental Italy and the islands of Sicily and Sardinia. U.S., Congress, Senate. *Senate Documents. Vol. 12. Emigration Conditions in Italy. Reports of the Immigration Commission.* Sen. Doc. 748, 61st Cong., 3rd sess., 1911, p. 141.

TABLE IV. Italian-Language Newspapers in Texas.

Newspaper	Place of Publication	Dates of Publication
La Tribuna Italiana	Dallas	1914-1963
Il Messaggiero Italiano	Galveston and San Antonio	1906-1914
La Patria degli Italiani	Galveston	1925-1925
La Stella del Texas	Galveston	1913-1918
L'Aurora	Houston	1906-1919
L'America	Houston	1925-1925
La Voce Patria	San Antonio	1925-1925

Source: "Italian-Language Newspapers in Texas," by Samuel J. Marino, Texas Woman's University (1981).

SAILING SHIPS. Typical of those built by Italian shipbuilders for Luis de Moscoso de Alvarado.

— Courtesy Texas State Library, Austin, Texas

ITALIANS IN TEXAS HISTORY
BEFORE THE CIVIL WAR

O we can wait no longer,
We too take ship O soul
Joyous we too launch out on trackless seas,
Fearless for unknown shores on waves of
ecstasy to sail.

— *Walt Whitman*

INTRODUCTION

In order to understand the dynamics of the roles played by Italians in early Texas history, it is necessary to take into account the close relationships between Spain and France with the states of the Italian peninsula during this period. In 1494 France put forward long-standing claims to Milan and Naples. When Spain intervened on Naples' behalf, Italy became a battleground for the protracted rivalry between France and the Habsburgs. Charles V, Holy Roman emperor and king of Spain, subsequently forged a defensive arc-sweeping from Spain through Italy to Germany and the Low Countries — to contain France, ensuring Spanish Habsburg dominance in Italy for nearly 200 years. Milan and Naples became part of the Spanish crown and other Italian states its satellites. The house of Bourbon-Spain began in 1700 with the accession of Philip V to the Spanish throne. Upon the conclusion of the War of the Spanish Succession (1701-14), Austria replaced Spain as the dominant foreign power in northern Italy. A Bourbon king was put on the Neapolitan throne, but Lombardy (Milan) was retained in the Habsburg dominions. The Kingdom of The Two Sicilies, as Naples-Sicily was styled, entered into a family compact with France and Spain. Bourbon-Sicily sprang from the Spanish line, and was founded in 1759 by Ferdinand I.

Napoleon Bonaparte's spectacular Italian campaigns in 1797 and 1799 shattered Austrian hegemony, drove the Bourbon king of the Two Sicilies from the mainland, and ended the 1,200-year history of the Venetian republic. By 1806 Napoleon — now emperor — had annexed large portions of Italy, including Rome, Piedmont, and Venetian possessions in Dalmatia, to France; deeded Naples to his brother-in-law, Marshal Joachim Murat; and created the Kingdom of Italy in northern and central Italy, naming himself its king. In the reactionary atmosphere that attended Napoleon's defeat, nationalism seemed a dangerous corollary of the French Revolution. Governments represented at the Congress of Vienna (1815) were intent on reviving the prerevolutionary equilibrium of a Europe torn by a generation of war. Old boundaries and old rulers were restored and their security guaranteed by the great powers. Lombardy-Venetia was returned to Austria, which also counted the satellite states — Tuscany, Modena, and Parma — within its sphere of influence. The Bourbons were restored to Naples and the pope to Rome. Only Piedmont stood outside the circle of foreign control or influence. Given the close relationships between France and Spain with the states of the Italian peninsula, it should not be surprising that there were prominent Italians among the Spaniards and Frenchmen who came to Texas.

ITALIAN EXPLORERS

Italians were on their way to Texas almost as soon as Europeans began sailing the Atlantic in search of a route to the Indies. A large statue of Christopher Columbus stands in Columbus Park at West Martin and Columbus Street in San Antonio. Although the daring,

New World explorer never visited Texas, in 1492 he led
one of the most important expeditions in the history of
humankind. It started the exploration, conquest, and
settlement of this new-found land, including Texas. Columbus called the New World inhabitants Indians, and
the name persisted. Columbus also brought the first cattle to the New World in 1493, on his second voyage, and
later conquistadores took them to every corner of Spain's
American empire. The city of Columbus, Texas, in Colorado County, is named in his honor. Most Americans are
aware that their country was named after the Italian,
Amerigo Vespucci. But few people realize that he and
others on his voyage in 1497 were the first known Europeans to see the present coast of Texas.[1] In a letter to
Don Ferdinand of Spain, Vespucci wrote that he and his
crew ". . . left the port of Cadiz on the 10th of May 1497,
and . . . took our way for the Great Gulf of Ocean Sea, on
which voyage I was engaged for eighteen months, dis-
covering a great extent of mainland, . . ."[2] This observa-
tion is readily confirmed by the European maps which
followed. These indicate the outline of Florida and the
Gulf of Mexico.

On March 7, 1539, Fray Marcos de Niza (Fra Marco
da Nizza), of Nizza, Italy, accompanied by another Italian friar named Onorato, set out from Mexico City to ex-
plore the land north of present Mexico. For weeks Fra
Marco journeyed through northern Mexico, and crossed
into the present United States somewhere in eastern Arizona. When the friar returned to Mexico City he helped
to inspire the formation of a magnificent expedition
northward under the command of Francisco Vasquez de
Coronado.[3] It was on February 23, 1540, that Coronado

---

[1] The University of Texas at San Antonio, Institute of Texan Cultures, *The Italian Texans.* San Antonio, Texas, 1973, p. 2.

[2] Clements R. Markham, *The Letters of Amerigo Vespucci.* (London: Hakluyt Society, 1894), p. 3.

[3] Giovanni Schiavo, *Four Centuries of Italian-American History.*
(New York: Vigo, 1955), pp. 65-66.

left from Compostela at the head of 225 horsemen and sixty infantrymen. They trekked into new Mexico and across the panhandles of Texas and Oklahoma into Kansas.[4] Fra Marco was with them, as was Francisco Rojo Loro of Sicily, who brought his own arms and horses with him; and two other Italians named Bartolome Napolitano and Marco Romano.[5] Thus, Italians were among the earliest Europeans to set foot on Texas soil. They helped Coronado to pave the way for many future explorations and an eventual Spanish foothold in the American southwest.

Hernando De Soto, a Spanish conquistador, explored (1539-1542) the present southeastern United States from Florida to Tennessee to Oklahoma in an unsuccessful search for treasure. On board one of his nine vessels was ". . . a Genoese shipbuilder who was to prove of great service."[6] Luis de Moscoso de Alvarado led an expedition from the Mississippi River into Texas, but it is not known if the Italian went with him. However, when Moscoso returned to the Mississippi, the Genoese directed the building of seven brigantines needed to navigate the river. ". . . the Genoese, the only person who knew how to construct the vessels, built the ships with the help of four or five Biscayan carpenters."[7] In 1543 the expedition descended the river in order to reach Mexico by sea. En route the ships were driven into the Texas coast by

[4] David Donoghue, "The Route of The Coronado Expedition in Texas," *Southwestern Historical Quarterly.* Vol. 30, No. 1, January 1929, pp. 181-192.

[5] Diccionario autobiografico de conquistadores y pobladores de Nueva Espana. Published by Francisco A. D. Icaza at Madrid in 1923, pp. 873-875; Juan de Cuebas, *The Muster Roll and Equipment of the Expedition of Francisco Vazquez De Coronado.* (Ann Arbor: William L. Clements Library, 1939), pp. 8, 12, 21. Although the surname "Romano," could be either Italian or Spanish, the forename "Marco" indicates that this explorer was Italian. The corresponding forename in Spanish is "Marcos."

[6] Carlos E. Casteneda, *Our Catholic Heritage in Texas 1519-1936.* Vol. I. (Austin: Von-Boeckmann-Jones, 1936), p. 119.

[7] *Ibid.,* p. 136.

ENRICO de TONTI with an Indian guide in East Texas.
— *Painting by Bruce Marshall*
— *Courtesy of The Institute of Texan Cultures*

bad weather, where they were forced to stay for two weeks. Certainly the Italian shipbuilder was with them.

Enrico Tonti was an early explorer of Texas. He was born at Gaeta, near Rome, about 1650. Although overshadowed by his commander, Robert Cavelier sieur de La Salle, Tonti left his own mark on Texas history. La Salle established a settlement on the Texas coast in 1685. When La Salle was reported missing, Tonti made one trip in search of him in 1686, and a second trip in 1689. These two attempts failed, but it was through the expeditions that Tonti's major contributions to Texas were made. In his writings, he gave the first accurate descriptions of the geography, inhabitants, and resources of the area. His data and sketches provided enough information for cartographers to make the first regional maps of the territory. Tonti, a great trailblazer, explored most of the southern part of the central United States, from Peoria to New Orleans and from Arkansas to Alabama. He helped to make possible the establishment of the new colony of Louisiana, and explored the entire Mississippi Valley.[8]

In 1764 the Marquis de Rubi was commissioned by the Spanish government to make an inspection of all the frontier settlements from Lower California to the Louisiana border. Rubi was the son of Francisco Pignatelli,[9] a Neapolitan, and one-time Spanish ambassador to France. Between August and November 1767 Rubi visited Texas. His recommendations were included in the royal order of 1772 entitled "New Regulations of the Presidios." They called for the abandonment of all Texas presidios and missions, except those at San Antonio and La Bahia.[10] This retrenchment was a military necessity brought on by Spanish failure to fend off the attacks of the western Apache in present Arizona and New Mexico, and those of the Comanche in Texas.[11] In August 1774 a group of 350 Spanish settlers from Los Adaes established a village on the San Antonio Road at the crossing of the Trinity River. The settlement was named Bucareli in honor of Viceroy Antonio Maria de Bucareli. Bucareli was of Florentine extraction, and he was probably the most outstanding viceroy in New Spain.

---

[8] For a complete survey of the explorations of Enrico Tonti, consult: Edmund R. Murphy, *Henry De Tonty: Fur Trader of the Mississippi.* (Baltimore: Johns Hopkins, 1941).

[9] Seymour Connor. *Texas in 1776: A Historical Description.* (Austin: Jenkins, 1975), p. 12; Enciclopedia Italiana Di Scienze, Lettere ed Arti, Istitvto Della Enciclopedia Italiana, Fondata Da Giovanni Treccani, Roma, 1949, pp. 268-270; It is not odd that an Italian was appointed as Spanish ambassador to France in the early 1700s. After the conclusion of the War of the Spanish Succession (1701-14), the Kingdom of the Two Sicilies, as Naples-Sicily was styled, entered into a family compact with France and Spain.

[10] Gerald Ashford, *Spanish Texas: Yesterday and Today.* (Austin: Pemberton, 1971), p. 161.

[11] Connor, *Texas in 1776: A Historical Description, op. cit.,* p. 12.

THE EARLIEST ITALIAN SETTLERS

A survey of the ethnic makeup of Spanish Texas from 1777 to 1793 shows two Italians living in the territory at that time. One resided in Nacogdoches, and the other in San Antonio.[12] Vicente Micheli was among the first Italian merchants to settle in Texas. A native of Brescia, he arrived in Nacogdoches in 1793. After 1806, Micheli moved to San Antonio where he became quite prosperous. He owned the Rancho de San Francisco, and later opened a general mercantile store. Micheli died in his adopted city of San Antonio in 1848.[13] In 1777, King Charles III of Spain gave orders for the admission of Spaniards, Italians, and Germans to Lower Louisiana for the purpose of cultivating the soil of that region. Some of these people immigrated to Texas shortly after France repossessed the Louisiana territory from Spain in 1800 and then sold it to the United States in 1803.[14]

Another Italian merchant to settle in San Antonio was Giuseppe Cassini. Cassini was born at San Remo in the Genoese republic in 1787. He came to America with a British passport dated 1816, which described him as an "inhabitant of Gibraltor *(sic)*." [15] In the mid-1820s he settled in San Antonio, established a general mercantile store, and began dealing extensively in real estate. When Ben Milam captured San Antonio from the Mexican forces in late 1835, Cassini furnished the Texans with food and supplies from the store. But Mexican troops looted his village and pillaged his home a few months

[12] Alicia V. Tjarks, "Comparative Demographic Analysis of Texas, 1777-1793," *Southwestern Historical Quarterly*, Vol. 77, No. 7, July 1973-1974, p. 325.

[13] The University of Texas at San Antonio, *The Italian Texans*, *op. cit.*, p. 5.

[14] Mattie Austin Hatcher, *The Opening of Texas To Foreign Settlement 1801-1821*. (Austin: University of Texas, 1927), pp. 11, 12, 192.

[15] Frederick C. Chabot, *San Antonio and its Beginnings*. (San Antonio: Naylor, 1931), pp. 118.

later, when General Lopez de Santa Anna drove all Texan sympathizers out of the area. When the Texan Revolution ended, Cassini returned to San Antonio and resumed dealing in real estate. He became wealthy, and died on January 1, 1862, while completing plans to buy the entire Mexican village of Piedras Negras.

After 1816 some Italians who had served as officers under Napoleon visited or settled in Texas. A few of them joined the colony established in 1818 by General Lallemand. Although the settlement failed, some of the settlers who had been affiliated with it remained in Texas.[16] From 1817 to 1820 the notorious pirate, Jean Lafitte, ruled Galveston, and was a power to be reckoned with by the conflicting forces trying to gain a foothold on the territory of Texas. Several Italian seamen are known to have served with Lafitte. For example, Captain Louis Chighizola of Genoa, and Captain Vincent Gambio were with Lafitte in the American line at the Battle of New Orleans (1815).[17] Although Chighizola and Gambio never made it to Galveston with Lafitte, it is highly probable that other Italian-Baratarians were with the group during their three-year stay at the island.

In 1842 Annibale Ranuzzi undoubtedly influenced many Italians to emigrate to Texas. He was born in Bologna, Italy, in 1810 and died there in 1866. A noted geographer, in 1842 Ranuzzi published the only Italian book about the Republic of Texas. His *Il Texas* portrays the state as a land of excitement, variety, and opportunity — extremely inviting to all foreigners and certainly to his own countrymen.[18] The Rev. Bartholomew Rolando,

[16] Frederick L. Olmsted, *A Journey Through Texas.* (New York: Burt Franklin, 1860), pp. 220-248; Schiavo, *Four Centuries of Italian-American History, op. cit.,* p. 168.

[17] Jane Lucas de Grummond, *The Baratarians And The Battle of New Orleans.* (Baton Rouge: Louisiana State University Press, 1961), pp. 4, 9, 105, 149, 155, 157.

[18] E. Ranuzzi cenami, *Il conte A.R.,* Firenze 1892, pp. 104-118; Giovanni Natali, *Un geografo bolognese: il conte A.R.,* Forli, 1917, pp. 72-84.

of the Lazarist missionary order, was the first Italian-
born missionary to come to Texas in 1845. He was born
in Bordighera, near Genoa, in 1812, and he came to
America in 1834. Fr. Rolando worked as assistant to the
Rev. John M. Odin, the priest who later became the first
bishop of Galveston — a diocese which included all of
Texas at that time. Father Rolando ministered in Houston in 1846, but he returned to Galveston the following
year and died there October 11. In November 1858, the
Rev. Francis Gatti was appointed rector of the college of
the Franciscan mission at Galveston. But in January
1859 he closed the college and moved to Philadelphia.[19]

During this period some anonymous promoter called
Texas the Italy of America, a comparison that was re-
peated by many writers, most of whom had never been
to Italy. They meant that the skies were usually sunny
and blue, the winters mild, and the summers mitigated
by cooling breezes.[20] Italy, Texas, in Ellis County, received its name for this reason.

ITALIANS INVOLVED IN THE
TEXAN REVOLUTION

During the Texan Revolution, Italian fought against
Italian, as men from Italy were in both armies. When General Lopez de Santa Anna came to Texas in 1836 to quell
the rebellion against Mexico, General Vicente Filisola was
with him as second-in-command. Born in Ravello, Italy, in
1789, Filisola migrated with his family to Spain, where he
joined the army in 1804. He was commissioned a second
lieutenant six years later. In 1811, Filisola was sent to
Mexico, where he eventually rose to the rank of general.
The most notable Italian to serve with the Texan army

[19] The University of Texas at San Antonio, *The Italian Texans,*
op. cit., pp. 5-6, 9; Giovanni Schiavo, *Italian-American History.* Vol.
II (New York: Vigo, 1949), pp. 382-383.

[20] Marilyn McAdams Sibley, *Travelers in Texas: 1761-1860.* (Austin: University of Texas Press, 1967), p. 54.

GENERAL VICENTE FILISOLA (2nd in command of Mexican troops in Texas)

— *Courtesy Prudhomme, C.L.; Album Mejicano.*
Mexico, C.L. Prudhomme, 1843

was Prospero Bernardi. Born in Italy in 1794, Bernardi immigrated to Texas early in 1836. On February 13, he enlisted with Captain Amasa Turner's New Orleans Volunteers.

At first, the war went badly for the Texans. From February 27 to March 2, units of the Mexican army killed most of Colonel F. W. Johnson's force of about 100 men in battles at San Patricio and Agua Dulce. Then the Alamo garrison of 183 Texans, commanded by Colonel W. B. Travis, fell on March 6. The Mexicans shot the few men who managed to survive the assault. The Goliad garrison surrendered two weeks later. Only one force remained to stop General Santa Anna's army of 7,500 men. A group of 1,500 armed Texans, commanded by General Sam Houston, withdrew before the Mexican advance directed against San Felipe until it reached the Brazos River. Houston established a fortified camp there on March 31, and awaited the advance of the enemy.

Ten days after the Texan army passed through San Felipe, Santa Anna arrived there on April 9. Filisola, with his column, came to San Felipe on the 15th. Filisola reported to the Mexican government that: "On the 15th, he (Sam Houston) . . . thought better to attack the president, (Santa Anna) because he was on the other side of the Brazos, unconnected with the other forces; he therefore sent the steamboat down the river to attract our attention, and marched against his Excellency." [21] Santa Anna dangerously overextended his forces as they chased across the prairies after Sam Houston's band of soldiers. Filisola and his troops were ordered to remain behind on the Brazos. Therefore, they were unable to rescue the emperor's forces from their massive defeat at San Jacinto on April 20 and 21. Before Houston would discuss peace terms with the captured Santa Anna, he required

[21] Colonel Andrew Jackson Houston, *The Sam Houston Campaign.* From Volume I of "The Texan Revolution," taken from the official orders and reports of his father, General Sam Houston, commanding the Texan army. (Houston: Gulfport, 1925), p. 7.

the Mexican leader to issue orders to Filisola, who was still on the Brazos, at Fort Bend, with the main Mexican army. The orders called on Filisola to immediately withdraw from the interior of Texas, to prevent his troops from committing depredations upon the inhabitants, and to release all Texas prisoners. In addition to the withdrawal orders, Santa Anna was also permitted to address the following personal note to Filisola:

(General Santa Anna to General Filisola)

My esteemed friend and comrade: As I am ignorant of the period I shall have to remain here, and you are retiring into the interior, I wish you to send me my equipage, that of my comrade, Almonte, that of Castrillon, that of Nunez, and a trunk of my secretary, Caro, which is in the chamber with those belonging to me, sending a confidential person with the muleteers and guide who will conduct them to this camp, and delivering him the enclosed safe conduct, that no accident may occur on the road.

I recommend to you to comply with my official orders, respecting the retreat of the troops, as early as possible. It is necessary for the security of the prisoners, and particularly for that of your affectionate friend and comrade.

ANTONIO LOPEZ DE SANTA ANNA.

San Jacinto, April 25, 1836.[22]

With the defeat of Santa Anna at San Jacinto, General Filisola became the commander of the Mexican army in Texas. Filisola faced a very difficult decision. Should he assault Houston's position in an effort to win the war for Mexico, and rescue the captured Mexican soldiers; or should he withdraw from Texas and leave Santa Anna and his men to the mercy of the enemy? After all, Santa Anna was in a situation of great duress and compelled to act against his will. Did his orders represent what he *really* wanted Filisola to do?

Filisola conferred with his generals and then decided

[22] *Ibid.,* p. 40.

to act in accordance with Santa Anna's instructions. He signed the Treaty of Velasco, and withdrew with his army into Mexico. Filisola's pamphlet, *Representacion Dirigida Al Supremo Gobierno En Defensa De Su Honor,* reveals that he was apparently sincere in his actions when he withdrew from Texas and recognized its independence.[23] But his decision was highly unpopular in Mexico. Santa Anna later criticized the Italian for obeying his own orders. According to Santa Anna: ". . . in my judgment, . . . the general that succeeded me in command . . . should have decided . . . to try an attack . . . It was not without surprise that I later heard the news of the retrograde movement so precipitately undertaken contrary to my real desire." [24] Other Mexican generals ridiculed Filisola, and attempted to make him a scapegoat for the disaster. He was relieved of his command, and arrested on July 15, 1840, on charges brought against him by General Jose Urrea. Almost a year passed before Filisola was successful in his defense and was freed.

A careful study of Filisola's *memoirs* reveals subtle evidence that the Italian was more sympathetic toward the Texan cause than is generally realized.[25] It was in keeping with his character to overtly or secretly champion the cause of oppressed people. When Agustín de Iturbide issued the call for Mexican independence from Spain on February 24, 1821, Filisola gave the pronouncement and Iturbide his wholehearted support. He fought at the Battle of Toluca, and when Iturbide entered Mexico City on September 27, 1821, to take command of the country and officially free the capital from the royalists, Filisola

[23] Gen. Vicente Filisola, *Representacion Dirigida Al Supremo Gobierno En Defensa De Su Honor.* (Mexico: Imprenta De Ignacio Cumplido, 1836).

[24] Gen. Antonio Lopez De Santa Anna, *Manifiesto Que De Sus Operaciones En La Campana De Tejas Y En Su Cautiverio Dirige A Sus Conciudadanos.* (Veracruz: Imprenta Liberal a cargo de Antonio Maria Valdes, 1837), p. 31.

[25] Don Vicente Filisola, *Memorias Para La Historia De La Guerra De Tejas.* (Mexico: Rafael, 1849), Vol. I, pp. 355-359.

was in command of over four thousand soldiers of the Trigarante army. As military governor of Central America, Filisola issued a decree on March 29, 1823, which released Central America from its ties with Mexico. When the Congress of Central America assembled on June 24 to install officers, the affair was "graced by the presence of Filisola." [26]

By May 1833, Filisola had established his headquarters at Matamoros. There he received Stephen F. Austin, the representative of the Texian Convention of 1833, who was going to present the grievances of the Texians to the Mexican government. Austin and Filisola visited together and seemingly came to an understanding on the status of Texas. After receiving a letter from Filisola dated May 17, 1833, Austin wrote to the Italian from Matamoros on May 30 that: "La contestacion que se sirvio V.E. dar a mi referida nota, con fecha 17, me ha llenado de satisfaccion, y esta enteramente en consonancia con el concepto que los habitantes de Tejas . . ." (The reply which your Excellency was kind enough to give my note, on the date of the 17th, filled me with satisfaction, and is in full agreement with the concepts of the inhabitants of Texas).[27]

On May 30, Austin also sent a letter to Captain Wiley Martin, in which he wrote that: "The Com. Gen'l Filisola is a . . . honest . . . soldier. His principles are liberal and republican . . . He thinks well of the idea of making a State of Texas, and has a good opinion of the colonists in general, . . ." [28] It is impossible to determine to what extent Filisola's decision to withdraw the Mexican army from Texas was knowingly or unwittingly in-

[26] James M. Day, *General Vicente Filisola, Evacuation of Texas.* (Waco: Texian Press, 1965), pp. iii-v.

[27] Austin to Filisola, Matamoros, May 30, 1833. *The Austin Papers.* Edited by Eugene C. Barker. Annual Report of the American Historical Association for the Year 1922. Vol. 2 (Washington, D.C.: U.S. Government Printing Office, 1928), p. 973.

[28] Austin to Wiley Martin, May 30, 1833, *The Austin Papers, op. cit.,* p. 977.

fluenced by his sympathy for the people of Texas in their struggle for independence. But his decision not to continue the campaign may have been a deciding factor in the outcome of the war. A military victory by Filisola over Houston after San Jacinto, would have altered the course of Texas history. According to Professor Seymour V. Connor, a leading scholar of Texas history, "Had Filisola, to whom the order was addressed, ... elected to ignore their captured commander and continue fighting, the future of Texas would have been entirely different. For with Houston incapacitated by his wound and the Texan army utterly disorganized by its amazing victory, it would not have been difficult for the Mexicans to have routed them. The odds were still six or seven to one. Filisola had withdrawn the Mexican armies to Matamoros where almost immediately he was ordered by Bustamante to reinvade Texas." [29] But Filisola vacillated and the invasion never took place.

Prospero Bernardi fought with the Texans at the Battle of San Jacinto. He served in Captain Turner's company and is listed among Sam Houston Dixon's *The Heroes of San Jacinto*. Discharged from active service on February 11, 1837, at Galveston, Bernardi received both a First Class grant and a Bounty grant for his gallant efforts on behalf of Texan independence. The First Class grant was for one-third league of land located in San Patricio County, and issued by the Board of Land Commissioners of Harrisburg County on February 10, 1838. The Bounty grant, issued on December 13, 1838, consisted of 1,280 acres on the southwest side of Paluxy Creek, nine miles from its junction with the Brazos River. The former grant states that Bernardi ". . . served faithfully and honorably for the term of eleven months from the 13th day of Feb. 1836 until the eleventh day of Feb. 1837

---

[29] Seymour V. Connor, *Texas: A History.* (Arlington Heights, Illinois: AHM Publishing Corporation, 1971), pp. 125-126, 118.

BATTLE OF SAN JACINTO with **Prospero Bernardi and Joseph Sovreign on battlefield.**

— *Painting by Bruce Marshall*
— *Courtesy of The Institute of Texan Cultures*

. . ." [30] A large bust of Prospero Bernardi stands in front of the Texas Hall of State, Fair Park, Dallas, Texas. What an imposing sight! Sculptured by Pompeo Coppini, the monument is five feet in height and rests upon an eighteen-foot base of Texas granite. Coppini portrayed Bernardi as having a well-muscled body, and dressed in a fringed, cotton and wool, frontier uniform. Bernardi's proud, erect stance and determined look give an impression of combat readiness. His right hand holds the handle of a short-barreled pistol, and his left hand grips the hilt of a long Bowie knife. An inscription on the

[30] Thomas Lloyd Miller, *Bounty and Donation Land Grants of Texas 1835-1888.* (Austin: University of Texas Press, 1967), p. 105. 1st Headright Certificate, cert. #294, Kleberg County, issued Feb. 10, 1838; registered and approved March 16, 1859. Certificate #5066, Somervill County, survey no. 12 of land entitled B. by certificate issued by the Board of Land Commissioners for Harrisburg County. Survey April 20, 1838. Sam Houston Dixon, *The Heroes of San Jacinto.* (Houston: Anson Jones, 1932), p. 110.

PROSPERO BERNARDI — Italian Texan Hero at
the Battle of San Jacinto — 1836.

base of the statue reads: PROSPERO BERNARDI —
ITALIAN TEXAN HERO AT THE BATTLE OF SAN
JACINTO — 1836.

The Bernardi monument was dedicated by Governor
James V. Allred on Columbus Day, October 12, 1936,
during the Texas Centennial Exposition. Dallas Mayor
George M. Sergeant, Commendatore Barlotomeo
Migone, first secretary to the Royal Italian Embassy in
Washington, D.C., and other dignitaries, attended the
unveiling ceremony and the commemorative banquet
held that evening. "Prospero Bernardi," Governor Allred said, "was one of the many unsung heroes, who
fought and gave their blood for Texas 100 years ago.
Some of them are known like Bernardi, others are unknown, but all live in the hearts of our people." Artist
Pompeo Coppini explained the circumstances involved
in his decision to work on the beautiful, bronze statue, in
his autobiography, *From Dawn to Sunset:* "In the months
that followed the completion of the Dallas statues, I kept

busy with three more interesting projects, one . . . was a commission from the Italian-American newspaper, *La Tribuna Italiana,* to make a heroic size portrait bust of Prospero Bernardi, who fought in the battle of San Jacinto with Sam Houston." [31] Bernardi was born in Italy in 1799, but virtually nothing is known about his early life. His honorable discharge from the Texian army states that in 1837 he was thirty-eight years of age, five feet eight-and-one-half inches tall, with dark complexion, dark eyes, and black hair. Bernardi's service record, signed by Captain John Smith, and approved by Secretary of War William L. Fisher, indicates that the Italian received a medical discharge because of a spinal injury sustained during combat against the Mexican army.

Other Italians also struggled for the independence of Texas. One of the most noteworthy was Orazio Donato Gideon de Attellis, Marquis of Sant'Angelo. Orazio de Attellis was born in Sant'Angelo Limosani (Molise) on October 22, 1774. On May 20, 1824, he arrived in America, and later he taught, wrote, and founded schools in New York and Mexico City. While in Mexico City, the marquis began a newspaper, called *El Correo Atlantico,* in which he advocated Texan independence. The Mexican government struck back immediately, and on June 25, 1835, the Italian was ordered to leave Mexico. He and his wife sailed from Vera Cruz to New Orleans, where he became openly, uncompromisingly, and completely dedicated to the cause of independence for Texas.[32]

Attellis continued printing his paper in New Or-

[31] Pompeo Coppini, *From Dawn to Sunset.* (San Antonio: Naylor, 1949), p. 365; *Dallas Guide and History.* Written and compiled by the Dallas unit of the Texas Writers' project of the Work Projects Administration, 1940, p. 630; Service Record No. 562, on file with the Dallas Historical Society, Library and Archives Research Center, Dallas, Texas. *Dallas Morning News,* October 12, 1936, Section II, pp. 1, 8; October 13, 1936, p. 1.

[32] Luciano G. Rusich, "Marquis of Sant'Angelo, Italian-American Patriot and Friend to Texas," *italian americana.* Vol. 5, no. 1, Fall/Winter, 1979, pp. 8-17.

leans, publicizing the Texan cause in Spanish, English, Italian, and French. He lashed out fiercely at the Mexican position. *The Telegraph and Texas Register* (August 23, 1836) called him "... a devoted friend of Texas ..." [33] The marquis also spoke at public meetings in an effort to raise money and enlist volunteers for Texas.[34] Finally, the Italian tried to arouse public opinion in Europe in favor of Texas by sending files to European newspapers.[35] On January 9, 1839, "the Senate and House of Representatives of the Republic of Texas in Congress assembled" donated "one league of land" to O. de A. Santangelo with the "thanks of Congress for the firm and zealous support with which he has maintained the cause of Texan independence in the periodical 'El Correo Atlantico' in opposition to the oppression of the enemies of civil and religious liberty." [36]

Giuseppe Cassiano was another Italian who strongly advocated that Texas should be liberated from Mexico. He was born in 1791 at San Remo, near Genoa (Liguria), on the Italian Riviera, the son of Geronimo Cassini and Catalina Cabassa. When he became an adult, Cassiano obtained a ship and acquired experience in sailing. He procured a British passport dated November 20, 1816,

[33] James E. Winston, "New Orleans Newspapers and the Texas Question, 1835-1837," *Southwestern Historical Quarterly.* Vol. 36, October 1932, p. 119.

[34] Charles A. Gulick Jr. (et al.) "O. de A. Santangelo Petition to the Honorable Congress of the Republic of Texas," *Lamar Papers,* II (Austin and New York: Pemberton, 1968), pp. 143-152.

[35] "George Fisher to Austin," *The Austin Papers.* III, p. 421.

[36] Copy of the joint resolution passed by the Congress of Texas, authenticated by the U.S. Consul in Marseilles on April 20, 1848, BNN: Ms VA 48/6. Part of the same authenticated document is a copy of the certificate issued by the Board of Land Commissioners of Harrisburg County and a sworn declaration by Santangelo stating that "although the land had been located on Survey No. 8 on the East side of the Colorado River by the Surveyors of Bastrop County, no such location was afterwards ascertained to have been made ..." and that the original certificate was lost by Charles F. Mayer, Esq., an attorney in charge of perfecting his rights on said land.

from the consul of Great Britain at Marseilles, and sailed to New Orleans. Cassiano moved to San Antonio and lived there during the period of Mexican sovereignty over Texas. On April 12, 1826, he married Donna Gertrudis Perez, the widow of Don Antonio Cordero y Bustamente, the military and political governor of Texas before Mexican independence. With an inheritance from her father and the great wealth of Cordero, added to Cassiano's vast possessions, they were easily the richest couple in the city of San Antonio. Giuseppe (Jose) Cassiano was openly sympathetic with, and very generous to, the movement for independence from Mexico.

According to Frederick C. Chabot, a scholar of early Texas history, "It is stated that he (Cassiano) made an important loan in cash to Sam Houston, and that he was most instrumental in financing the Texas war of independence. He did so much, in fact, that on June 21, 1836, Thomas J. Rusk, brigadier general in command, issued instructions to the appropriate authorities that Cassiano be permitted to embark aboard any vessel with his family, servants, and household effects, to return to New Orleans; and at the same time, that he be freely permitted to bring back into any of the ports, Galveston, Velasco, or Matagorda, any provisions or goods he might choose to import into Texas. In the winter of 1835, his home and store were given over to the Texas army when they took possession of San Antonio. Cassiano offered to present the government of the United States 500 A. of land situated on the Rio Grande, just opposite the Presidio del Rio Grande; this contract was signed in 1849 by E. B. Babbitt, Quartermaster of the U.S.A., and by Jose Cassiano; these signatures were witnessed by W. W. Harrison." [37] Giuseppe Cassiano became an American citizen

[37] Frederick C. Chabot, *With The Makers of San Antonio.* (San Antonio: Artes Graficas, 1937), p. 223; Evelyn M. Carrington, *Women in Early Texas.* (Austin: Jenkins, 1975), p. 56. Two interesting accounts of Giuseppe Cassiano and his family are published in the "S.A. Express," of August 30, 1936; and in the Texas Pioneer magazine, August 1930.

before his death on January 1, 1862. The financial aid that he rendered to Houston may have influenced the outcome of the Texas war of independence.

ITALIAN SETTLERS BETWEEN WARS

Upon receiving Houston's report of the victory at San Jacinto and the capture of General Santa Anna, President David G. Burnet and the *ad interim* government moved from Galveston Island to Velasco at the mouth of the Brazos. There on May 14th the two treaties of Velasco were signed by Burnet and Santa Anna. During the first fifteen months after the war, Texans strove to align themselves with the United States in order to assure their independence from Mexico. However, as the United States continued to display reluctance to annex the Republic, Texas officials felt compelled to seek aid from European sources. In 1839, Texan James Pinckney Henderson was in Paris on a diplomatic mission to obtain French recognition of Texas independence, and to negotiate favorable Texan-French trade relations. Henderson suggested to his superiors that a special envoy should be dispatched to approach "the different Powers of Europe which have not yet applied to for . . . recognition . . ." [38] In explaining his reasoning, Henderson maintained that in some of these European countries Texas might acquire a profitable market for its sugar. The Italian states were probably included in his plan, but there was no known formal contact between Texas officials and Italian leaders, and Texas was annexed to the United States in 1845.

In 1850 there were at least forty-one Italians living in Texas, exclusive of native Corsicans. By 1860 the figure was not much higher, with only sixty-seven reported. [39] A majority of the Italians were concentrated in

[38] Henderson to Secretary of State (Burnett), 5 August 1839, *TDC,* III 1266-1267.

[39] Data for 1850 from J.D.B. DeBow, either *The Seventh Census,* pp. 36-37, or *Compendium of the Seventh Census,* pp. 116-118; data

the larger river and coastal towns. A study of migration patterns of foreign-born Italians living in Texas before the Civil War demonstrates that most of them came directly from Europe, passing through one of the principal seaports, probably Galveston. There were, of course, exceptions. A number of Italians came through Louisiana, lived briefly there, and migrated to Texas. Galveston included in its 1860 population thirteen Italians,[40] and one of the thirty-one occupants of the city's Eagle Hotel that year was an Italian.[41] There were three Italians living in Ward 2 of Galveston, one of which was a barkeeper.[42] Meanwhile, a Brownsville hotel was operated by Italian-born C., Angelino.[43] In Houston in 1860 there were six Italians, one of whom was a clerk and another a bookkeeper.[44] There was an equal number of Italians living in Ward 1 of San Antonio. One of these people was a craftsman, another a merchant, a third a rancher, and a fourth a stage driver.[45]

Among the most notable Italians living in Texas at this time were Decimus et Ultimus Barziza, Father Augustine d'Asti, and Antonio Bruni. Barziza went to Texas in 1857 and rose to prominence there. His father was Viscount Filippo Ignacio, a Venetian who had settled at Williamsburg, Virginia, in 1814. Lawyer and banker, Decimus et Ultimus is remembered as the greatest criminal lawyer in Texas of his time, and as the author of a vivid Civil War memoir, titled *The Adventures of a Pris-*

---

for 1860 from *The Eighth Census*, 1860, Vol. I, Population, 490 or 616-623. The percents have been supplied.

[40] Based upon a study of the manuscript returns of Schedule No. 1, Free Inhabitants, of the United States Census, 1860. The originals of these returns are in the National Archives, Washington, D.C. The author used microfilm copies in the Institute of Texan Cultures, San Antonio, Texas.

[41] *Ibid.*, Galveston County, City of Galveston, 2nd Ward, 65-66.

[42] *Ibid.*

[43] *Ibid.*, Cameron County, City of Brownsville, 2nd Ward, 32.

[44] *Ibid.*, Harris County, City of Houston, 3rd Ward, 118.

[45] *Ibid.*, Bexar County, City of San Antonio, 1st Ward, 43.

FATHER AUGUSTINE D'ASTI, pastor of St. Vincent's Catholic Church, Houston, Texas.
— *Courtesy Annunciation Church Archives, Houston, Texas*

oner of War. He studied law in Baylor University at Independence, and then began a practice at Owensville, the old seat of Robertson County. The Civil War interrupted his career and he was commissioned a first lieutenant in Hood's Texas Brigade.[46] The brigade fought with the Army of Northern Virginia, participated in all major engagements, and sustained heavy casualties. Captured at Gettysburg, he was later imprisoned on Johnson's Is-

[46] Decimus et Ultimus Barziza, *The Adventures of a Prisoner of War 1863-1864.* Edited by R. Henderson, (Shuffler: Austin, 1964), pp. 1-18; "D.U. Barziza defends himself in Houston Ship Channel imbroglio, Barziza and the Breakwater," *Galveston News.* July 9, 1876, p.2.

land, but made a successful escape. After the war, Barziza resumed the practice of law in Houston. The oldest deed recorded in Montague County for a person of Italian lineage was for 200 acres of land purchased by him. Barziza bought the land from W. C. Wilson, also of Harris County, on January 19, 1871, for a sum of three hundred dollars.[47] Barziza turned briefly to politics and was elected to the 14th Legislature in 1873, the session which marked the end of Reconstruction rule in Texas. He resigned from the legislature in 1876, and died at his home on January 30, 1882. Today there is a Barziza Street in Houston.

Father Augustine d'Asti was born at St. Damiano d'Asti in Piedmont. In 1860, Bishop Odin of Galveston requested that the Franciscans reestablish themselves in Texas, where they had not been since the revolution of 1836. Father Augustine became pastor of St. Vincent's Catholic Church in Civil War Houston. He distributed food, clothing, and money among the needy people of the city. Today, d'Asti House at 603 Irvine Street carries on the charitable tradition of this compassionate Italian priest by dispensing similar gifts each day to the needy people of Houston. Father Augustine is also remembered for having blessed the flag which Dick Dowling and his men carried into the battles of Galveston and Sabine Pass.[48]

Antonio Bruni — a San Antonio businessman, politician, and public benefactor — was encouraged by his own success to invite other Italians to settle in Texas. He left his native Italy in 1858, landed at Galveston, then proceeded to San Antonio, where he prospered. His political career began in 1879 when he was elected alderman. He also served as Market Master in the 1880s. His nephew, Antonio Mateo Bruni, was a dominant business and po-

[47] Texas, Montague County, Deed Record Volume C., pp. 118-119; Reverse Index to Deeds, A-K, 1-2-3, p. 22.

[48] The Institute of Texan Cultures, *The Italian Texans, op. cit.,* pp 9-11.

litical figure in South Texas for a quarter of a century. The town of Bruni was established on one of the ranches of Antonio Mateo to provide a shipping point for his agricultural produce, and his memory is also perpetuated in Bruni Park at Laredo.[49]

CONCLUSION

Early Italian explorers and settlers helped to found and develop Texas. The 1539 trip of Fra Marco da Nizza was especially important. The Coronado expedition of 1450 moved northward "on his footprints." His journey helped to initiate the European exploration and colonization of what was to later become the southwestern part of the United States, including Texas. While most people are aware of the impact of Italians on American civilization as a late 19th and 20th century phenomenon, and one that focused on the eastern portions of the United States, the role of Italians in Texas prior to 1861 is not generally known.

The original Italian settlers acquainted other Italians with the agricultural and economic opportunities of the territory, and were the forerunners of the nineteenth century rural Italian settlements in Montague County, the Brazos Valley, and on the Galveston County mainland. They were also the forerunners of the major urban settlements of Houston, Galveston, and San Antonio. They serve as a source of pride and inspiration for modern Italian Texans, and are a means by which to help later settlers to more easily identify with the heritage of the state. The strength and dedication of Italians contributed much, in proportion to their numbers, to the history of Texas before the Civil War. This fact should be pointed out in books which deal with this period of Texas history.

[49] *New Encyclopedia of Texas.* Vol. IV, 1929, p. 2756; A. M. Bruni, *History of Southwest Texas.* Vol. II, 1907, State Archives, pp. 96, 97; Edward W. Heusinger, *The Heusinger Family in Texas.* (San Antonio: University of Texas, 1945), pp. 57-62.

EXTERIOR OF Frank Pizzini Store. San Antonio, Texas.
— *Courtesy Henry Guerra, San Antonio, Texas*
Copy From U.T. Institute of Texan Cultures,
San Antonio, Texas

URBAN ITALIAN SETTLEMENTS
IN TEXAS: 1880-1920

And they (methinks) deserve my pity,
Who for it can endure the stings,
The crowd, and buz, and murmurings of
this great hive, the city.
                    — *Abraham Cowley.*

Between 1880 and 1920 most Italians in Texas were employed as farmers or miners. But many of them also lived and worked in urban areas. Some of the Italians who lived in Texas cities during this period had been tradesmen in Italy, while others were former cotton farmers in the state. In 1898, after a decade of declining prices, the New York Cotton Exchange reached the lowest point in history at less than five cents a pound. A number of Texas farmers turned to other crops, or abandoned farming to become merchants or laborers in the expanding urban centers of Texas. Italian farmers were among them. Giuseppe Degelia had been a cotton farmer in Brazos county since his family moved there from Louisiana in 1887. But in 1915 Giuseppe moved his family to Dallas to enter the grocery business. According to his son, John Degelia, "The price of cotton dropped too low to allow the small farmer to make a profit." [1] By 1900, one-third of all Italian Texans lived in urban areas. [2] Dal-

---

[1] Robert L. Brandfon, *Cotton Kingdom of the New South.* (Cambridge: Harvard, 1967), p. 146. John Degelia, private interview held at 5305 Dazzle, Dallas, Texas, February 20, 1982.

[2] United States Census Office, Twelfth Census of the United States, 1900, Population, Part I, Washington, D.C., 1903, pp. 783-786.

las, San Antonio, Houston, and Galveston had significant numbers of them. Table V shows the number of foreign-born Italians residing in these cities between 1890 and 1920. The Table indicates an increase in the Italian population every decade during this time period. Italians migrated to these cities, and also to Beaumont, Waco, and Fort Worth in search of economic opportunities.

TABLE V. Major Urban Settlements of
Italian-Texans: 1890-1920.

City	Total Population				Number of Italians			
	1890	1900	1910	1920	1890	1900	1910	1920
Dallas	38,067	42,638	92,104	158,976	161	167	338	584
Galveston	29,084	37,789	36,981	44,255	225	566	568	693
Houston	27,557	44,633	78,000	138,276	196	352	639	1,300
San Antonio	37,673	53,321	96,614	161,379	245	264	444	601
Total	132,281	178,381	303,699	502,886	827	1,349	1,989	3,178

Sources: Compendium of the Eleventh Census of the United States. Vol. III
(Washington, 1894), pp. 672-675.

Twelfth Census of the United States, Vol. I (Washington, 1903), pp.
798-803.

Thirteenth Census of the United States. Vol. III (Washington,
1913), pp. 852-859.

Fourteenth Census of the United States. Vol. III (Washington,
1922), p. 1024.

The Italian government was very interested in the welfare of the Italian Texans, most of whom remained proud of their heritage. When Italian Ambassador Edmondo Mayor des Planches visited Houston, Dallas, and San Antonio in 1905, enthusiastic crowds displaying the Italian colors greeted him at the train stations. On April 26, a fervid welcome by more than 1,000 persons met him in Houston.[3] The ambassador was very impressed by the accomplishments of his countrymen, and he gave special praise to Giovanni Beretta, an Italian banker at San Antonio, who owned more than 100,000 acres of land along the Rio Grande River near Laredo.[4] At that

[3] *Galveston Daily News,* April 27, 1905, p. 12.

[4] Edmondo Mayor des Planches, *Attraverso gli Stati Uniti Per L'emigrazione italiana.* (Torino: Unione tipografico-editrice torinese, 1913), p. 189.

time Italians were engaged in several different urban occupations in Texas. The most popular field for them was
small business — retail grocery, fruits and confectionary,
and boot and shoe making. Table VI shows the number
of Italians involved in these occupations in 1906. The experiences of Salvatore Lucchese and Francesco Talerico
were typical.

TABLE VI. Major Occupations of
Urban Italian-Texans: 1906.

City	Total Number of Business Establishments			Number of Italian-Owned Businesses		
	Retail Grocery	Confectionary & Fruits	Shoe-making	Retail Grocery	Confectionary & Fruits	Shoe-making
Dallas	310	45	49	28 (9%)	10 (22%)	5 (10%)
San Antonio	324	48	52	39 (12%)	14 (29%)	7 (13%)
Galveston	188	16	24	94 (50%)	4 (25%)	6 (25%)
Houston	440	35	38	57 (13%)	4 (11%)	14 (37%)
Beaumont	112	30	15	32 (28%)	9 (30%)	10 (67%)
Total	1,374	174	178	250 (18%)	41 (24%)	42 (24%)

Sources: Dallas, San Antonio, Galveston, Houston and Beaumont City Directories (1906), Rosenberg Library,
Houston Public Library, Dallas Public Library, and
the San Antonio Public Library.

Francesco Talerico was born at Spezzano della Sila
in the province of Cosenza (Calabria) in 1860. He arrived
in San Antonio in 1888 by way of New York, and opened
a fruit stand in the business district. In a short time he
owned fifteen such stands, all operated by friends and
relatives from his native village. He organized the small
Italian community at San Antonio, and died in that city
in 1934. Michele Rizzo was one of the Italians who was
inspired to come to San Antonio by Talerico's success.
Born at Spezzano della Sila in 1899, Rizzo arrived in New
York on December 31, 1913, and then he moved to San
Antonio in 1922. For many years he operated a successful produce business there.[5]

   [5] Michele Rizzo, private interview held at Christopher Columbus
Hall, 201 Morales Street, San Antonio, Texas, June 1, 1980.

FRANK PIZZINI Family Reunion, August 15, 1913

— Courtesy Henry Guerra (San Antonio, Texas)
Copy From U.T. Institute of Texan Cultures,

Salvatore Lucchese was born into a bootmaking family near Palermo, Sicily in 1866. He sailed to Galveston in 1882, and settled at San Antonio a year later, when he opened a boot shop. The business grew until he became one of the best known custom boot makers in the United States. Lucchese made boots for Theodore Roosevelt in 1898, and for Francisco Madero, leader of the Mexican Revolution. The Italian died in San Antonio in 1929.[6] Most of the Sicilians who migrated to Texas were from villages near Palermo and Trapani on the northwest coast of Sicily. A majority of the Calabrians who settled in San Antonio came from Cosenza, which is located in the western part of the region.

Groceries, fruit dealerships, and shoemaking were sensible businesses for ambitious Italian immigrants to enter, because these fields required relatively small amounts of training and initial capital. But other occupations also provided opportunities. For example, many urban Italians owned saloons which served only beer and wine. There were also a number of clerks, sales people and bookkeepers, and quite a few barbers of Italian descent working in Texas cities in 1906. That year, between ten and fifteen percent of the barbers in Galveston,. San Antonio, Houston, and Beaumont, but only three percent of the barbers in Dallas were of Italian lineage.[7] Sometimes, the success of Italians in a particular occupation was limited to a single city. In Beaumont, one-fourth of the meat markets (twelve of forty-nine) were operated by Italians, but in other Texas cities there were only a few Italian-owned markets. Francesco Liberto was the proprietor of a large business of this kind in Beaumont. Liberto was born in Sicily in 1890. He emigrated to New Orleans and opened a small grocery store

[6] Sam Lucchese, private interview held at Christopher Columbus Hall, 201 Morales Street, San Antonio, Texas, June 1, 1980.

[7] Dallas, Galveston, San Antonio, Houston, and Beaumont, *City Directories* (1906). Rosenberg Library, Houston Public Library, Dallas Public Library, and San Antonio Public Library.

SAM LIBERTO GROCERY. San Antonio. Left to right: Sam, Enrico, and Angelina Liberto.
— *Courtesy Sam Liberto.*
Copy From U.T. Institute of Texan Cultures,

there, and then in 1899, he moved to Beaumont and established the Crescent City Market on the Houston highway. Liberto helped organize the San Salvadore Society, which assisted newly arrived immigrants in finding jobs, loaned them money to start businesses, and even provided burial expenses for its members. He died in San Antonio in 1940.[8]

Galveston offered opportunities in fishing. In 1906, more than ten percent of the Italians living there were fishermen or employed in port-related activities.[9] Luigi Cobolini was born in Trieste in 1845. He came to Galveston in 1867, where he peddled fish and fruit on the streets. He grew prosperous and soon acquired his own fishing schooner, the *Henry Williams.* Cobolini became a leader of the Galveston fishing industry and established fisheries at other points along the Texas Gulf Coast. He took an active part in the organization of Texas labor, and in 1894 he was elected as president of the State Federation of Labor. After twenty-six years in Galveston, Cobolini moved to Rockport, and then to Brownsville in 1907. During the early 1920s, this Italian Texan served on the Brownsville city commission. He died in that city in 1928.[10]

There were relatively few laborers among urban Italian Texans. According to the various city directories for 1906, twelve percent of the Italians living in Galveston were classified as laborers, and the figure for the other four cities under study was less than six percent. The Galveston list of registered voters for that year lists "merchant" as the occupation for more than half of the Italians recorded,[11] whereas, thirty-three percent of the Italians who declared their intention to become United States citizens in 1906 and 1907 were classified as labor-

[8] The Institute of Texan Cultures, *The Italian Texans.* (San Antonio: University of Texas, 1973), p. 22.

[9] *Galveston City Directory* (1906), p. 324.

[10] *The Italian Texans, op. cit.,* pp. 21-22.

[11] Poll Tax Record (1906), Galveston County Clerk's Office.

ITALIAN SHRIMP BOATS. Galveston, Texas
— *Courtesy of U.T. Institute of Texan Cultures*
San Antonio, Texas

ers.[12] Table VII compares the number of Italian laborers applying for American citizenship with the number of laborers for six other national groups between 1906-1907. The Table demonstrates that all of the other nationalities had a higher percentage of laborers applying for citizenship than the Italians, and that the percentage figure for Italian laborers (33%), was about half the percentage of the average for all of the groups (65%).

TABLE VII. Number of Laborers Applying for United States Citizenship Among Seven National Groups: Galveston (1906-1907).

Nationality	No. of Applicants	No. of Laborers
Montenegrans	24	24 (100%)
Austrians	63	53 (84%)
Hungarians	22	18 (82%)
Russians	48	37 (77%)
Germans	54	27 (50%)
Norwegians	23	10 (43%)
Italians	51	17 (33%)
Total	285	186 (65%)

Source: Declaration of Intent to Become a Citizen (1906-1907). District Clerk's Office, Galveston, Texas.

There were also relatively few professionals among urban Italian Texans in early twentieth century Texas. This is understandable. Italian professionals experienced language and professional licensure problems in America. These barriers forced many of them either to settle in an Italian community, or to find some kind of unskilled employment. Within the major urban centers of Texas in 1906, there was only one dentist with an Italian surname in Houston; one teacher in Houston and Beaumont; one osteopath and druggist in Dallas; and no

[12] Declaration of Intent to Become a Citizen (1906-1907). District Clerk's Office, Galveston, Texas.

lawyers.[13] But with a growing familiarity with the English language and acculturation into the dominant culture, Italians in time came to take their place among professional groups at the highest level. They became physicians, attorneys, corporation executives, and military leaders. Vincenzo Chiodo was born in Alia, Sicily, on January 10, 1892, the son of Salvatore and Asanta Chiodo. The Chiodo family moved to New Orleans before Vincenzo was one year old, and then they moved again, this time to Houston in 1893. After his graduation from high school and Massey Business College, Vincenzo entered the insurance business and was active in that profession for more than forty-two years. He was a member of the National Guard and of the State Guard of Texas for thirty-nine years, and served as a group commander of the State Guard. Chiodo achieved the rank of major general, and commanded the 36th Division in World War I. He personally recruited 197 men for active military service during that war. General Chiodo married Theresa R. Rabito, and the couple had three children.[14]

Many Italians attempted to adapt the nonurban institutions and culture they were familiar with in their native villages to the urban milieu in Texas. The rural lifestyle was not only discernible in new forms, but much of its original structure was intact. The importance of the family, the immigrant church, the Italian language press, and benevolent-fraternal organizations which played important roles in rural Italy were often adopted and adapted to the urban communities. Urban Italians viewed the world from the family circle, and considered everything outside it as either a means to its maintenance or to its destruction. While the outside world was used for the benefit of the family, it was faced with detachment and sometimes hostility in most other

[13] Dallas, Galveston, San Antonio, Houston, and Beaumont, *City Directories* (1906).

[14] Vincenzo Chiodo, private interview held at 1300 S. Lamar Street, Houston, Texas, July 6, 1980.

respects. Whenever possible, work was sought within establishments connected to the family circle. When this was not possible, work was primarily a means of obtaining income to assure the well-being of the family. The type of work, success, and economic advancement — while not absolutely rejected — were of secondary priority to the life that went on within the family circle.[15]

The Italians of Dallas were especially dependent upon their extended families to provide for individual needs because there was no concentrated ethnic community in that city from which they could draw upon for mutual support. Individual families were scattered throughout the city. But family units were very strong, and divorce was virtually unknown. Wives and children worked with the men in small family businesses, and living quarters were usually connected to the places of employment or located nearby. The largest group of Italians living in Dallas in 1906 were Sicilians who emigrated to Texas *via* New Orleans or New York. They worshipped at the St. Patrick Catholic Church, and the Sacred Heart Catholic Church along with Irish and German Catholics, and other ethnic groups. There was only a small number of Mexicans living in Dallas at that time. Entertainment for Italian Dallasites consisted primarily of dinners and parties held at home, or the homes of friends, and Italian games such as *bocce* and *briscola*. In the 1920s, the men formed a mutual aid society known as the *Zuroma Lodge,* and the Dallas-based newspaper *La Tribuna Italiana* was very popular with Italians living in the city after 1913.[16]

Italians often came to Dallas only after their families had settled in other parts of the state and/or country, and therefore they were partially acculturated when

[15] For a thorough discussion of the importance of the family to working-class Italian Americans consult: Herbert J. Gans, *The Urban Villagers.* (New York: The Free Press, 1962), pp. 229-261.

[16] Raymond Terranella, private interview held at 4501 Belclaire, Dallas, Texas, January 18, 1982.

VINCENT RINANDO'S Alamo Grocery Store, Beaumont, Texas 1919
— Courtesy Sam Liberto, San Antonio, Texas
Copy From U.T. Institute of Texan Cultures,
San Antonio, Texas

A. P. (Tony the Rep.) Fenoglio (3rd from left); Anthony H. (Tonicho) Fenoglio (with folding rule); Fill Fenoglio (kneeling on right). Judging game of bocce.

— Courtesy Fill Fenoglio, Montague, Texas
Copy From U.T. Institute of Texan Cultures,

AN ENGLISH language edition of the newspaper,
La Tribuna Italiana.

they arrived in the city. Vicente Chimento was the first
of his family to move to Waco, Texas, from Alia, Sicily,
in 1889. He was the son of Domenico Chimento and Rosalia Barcelona. About the same time, Gaetano Barcelona, Rosalia's brother, emigrated to San Antonio and
opened a pickle factory. The two men independently sailed
from Palermo to New York, and remained with relatives
in Brooklyn for awhile. Then they sailed to Galveston
and traveled overland to their respective destinations.
They were encouraged to come to Texas by friends and
relatives who had already settled there. Chimento became the owner of several wholesale houses in Waco. He
changed his name to Vince Kemendo and his business
was known as V. Kemendo and sons. After they had become established, Kemendo and Barcelona sponsored
the passage of several other members of their family to

America. Vicente's son, Toledo Kemendo, was born in Alia in 1884, but he moved with his family to Waco when he was five years old. Toledo was a polished Shakespearean recitalist who happened to make his living as a barber at the old Texas Bank Building Barber Shop. He had moved to Dallas from Waco in the late 1920s. Toledo appeared in many productions for the Dallas Little Theater, the Oak Cliff Little Theater, and the Footlights Club. He died in Dallas on July 11, 1969.[17]

Italians who had previously lived in other parts of the state and/or country also settled in Fort Worth. People from Liguria, Sicily, and Campania came to Texas *via* New York and New Orleans, and established homes in Fort Worth and in Tarrant County south of that city. Most Italians who settled in Fort Worth lived in the eastern part of the city. They opened small businesses, worshipped at the St. Patrick Catholic Church, and read *La Tribuna Italiana.* The men formed the Amita Club and some of them achieved prominent status. For example, Giovanni Laneri was an important real estate investor during the 1920s. For a time he served as director of the Fort Worth National Bank. A wealthy philanthropist, Laneri donated large sums of money to local churches and schools, and to humanitarian causes. Laneri Street in Dallas is named in his honor.[18]

The Catholic Church was an important formal institution to many urban Italian Texans. The church provided these people with a facility for religious worship, and in some instances, for the parochial education of their children. Even so, Italians living in Texas were not closely identified with the churches they attended. Southern Italians, especially Sicilians, were traditionally anticlerical because the Catholic Church, in the past, had sided with the large landowners against the peasants

[17] Bernard L. Kemendo, private interview held at 5641 Yale Blvd., Dallas, Texas, January 23, 1982.

[18] John and Rose Laneri, private interview held at 804 Havenwood, Fort Worth, Texas, January 20, 1982.

and farm laborers. The tradition of nonidentification with the church continued for some time in America. Nevertheless, at the turn of the century, most Italian Texans were a religious people, and they accepted nearly all of the moral norms and sacred symbols of the Catholic Church. Thus, they identified with the religion, but not with the church, except when it functioned as a moral agency. In his moral role, the priest was greatly respected. He served as judge and jury on all religious matters and on moral transgressions. The Italian community also had considerable respect for nuns. Because of their virginity and their total dedication to whatever duty they were assigned by the male leadership of the dioceses, nuns implemented to perfection the male ideal of *serietá* (seriousness), or the fine woman.[19]

Nonidentification of Italians with the local churches was also due to the fact that between 1841-1956 the hierarchy of the Catholic Church in Texas was predominantly Irish.[20] The Irish and Italians have different concepts of the Catholic religion. For example, Italian Catholicism emphasizes the worship of the Virgin Mary, whereas, Irish Catholicism stresses, among other things, the Trinity. Even so, Italians were not visibly bothered by the dominance of the Irish, if only because the church did not really engage them strongly. Some Italians attended services at Mexican churches because their arrangements and rituals more closely resembled the village churches in Italy.

In some instances, Italian Texans formed ethnic churches, or maintained religious practices common in their native Italy. Ethnic churches existed in San Antonio and in Galveston. In 1927 the Christopher Columbus Italian Society of San Antonio donated land for the

[19] For a thorough discussion of the ideal of womanliness in traditional Italian culture consult: Richard Gambino, *Blood of my Blood.* (New York: Anchor, 1975), pp. 160-182.

[20] Carlos E. Castaneda, *Our Catholic Heritage in Texas.* Volume VII. (New York: Arno Press, 1969), pp. 477-490.

ST. JOSEPH'S ALTAR (Location unknown)
— *Courtesy of U.T. Institute of Texan Cultures*
San Antonio, Texas

building of the Italian community church of San Francesco Di Paola. Two yeas later, in May 1929, Italian-speaking Protestants, primarily from Tuscany, organized the Valdese Presbyterian Church in Galveston with thirty-five charter members. Services were bilingual. Older members generally attended Italian language masses, while younger people participated in the English language services.

The custom of celebrating, on March 19, the Feast of St. Joseph — with the St. Joseph altar, or table — was widely practiced by Sicilian Catholics living in Texas cities. Since the feast was held during Lent, it had to be

ST. JOSEPH'S Catholic Church, Beaumont, Texas
— Courtesy Sam Liberto, San Antonio, Texas
— Copy From U.T. Institute of Texan Cultures,
San Antonio, Texas

prepared without meat. For this important event preparations were made weeks in advance. An altar was erected at the end of a large room against a background of white satin, and in the center was placed a life-size statue of St. Joseph holding the hand of the Baby Jesus with the proud mother watching them. Tall white tapers and waxy white Easter lilies surrounded the statues. A long table the length of the room was laden with food of every description. A group of people was selected from poor families and orphans to represent the Holy Family. After the representatives of the Holy Family and a number of little girls acting as angels were seated, a priest entered the room and blessed all before him. Then a little boy, taking the part of the Infant Jesus, who had been taught to bless all around him with his two fingers, raised his hand in benediction, and the dinner began. First, one segment of orange was served to each person at the table. This was followed by lentil soup, spaghetti Milanese, fish, frittata, artichokes, burdock, finocchio, olives, pickles, salads, cheeses, eggs, vegetables, fruits, cookies of every description, and breads made in many creative shapes and styles. Finally, confetti with almond, confetti with liquor, wines, and milk were served at the end of the feast. Then the guests, who had been praying and singing religious songs, were invited to eat, continuing the festivity until a late hour. The guests leave laden with food and memories of a great event.

The Italian language press was important to literate Italian immigrants living in urban Texas. Before the turn of the century, they subscribed to newspapers printed in Italy, New York, Chicago, San Francisco, or New Orleans. Then in September, 1906, *Il Messaggiero Italiano* (1906-1913), the first Italian language newspaper in Texas, was introduced in Galveston. The weekly publication emphasized national and international news, and displayed advertisements of Houston and Galveston businesses. At first, the readership was largely limited to Italians living in the Houston-Galveston area. But in 1907, the paper

SAN FRANCESCO de Paola Church, San Antonio, Texas
*— Courtesy Father Henry Herrera, San Antonio
Copy From U.T. Institute of Texan Cultures,*

was consolidated with *L'America*, another Italian language newspaper of Chicago. *Il Messaggiero Italiano* was moved to San Antonio, but its Chicago and Galveston advertisements mostly remained. The last known copy is dated December 27, 1913. The only other Italian language newspaper in San Antonio was *La Voce Patria*, published for a few months in 1925, and limited in scope to news about Italy and local Italians.[21]

A Galveston newspaper, titled *La Stella del Texas*, began publication in 1913, and had a circulation of about 20,000.[22] It presented extensive social news, East Texas real estate deals, and political advertising during elections. Publication of the newspaper ceased in 1918. The short-lived, Galveston-based *La Patria degli Italiani* (1925) offered national and international news to its readership.[23] Houston hosted two Italian language weeklies, *L'Aurora* (1906, 1911-1923), and *L'America*, which was published for only a few months in 1925.[24] Both of them contained local, national, and international news events of interest to Italian Americans. The heyday of Italian newspapers in Texas spanned only a few years, from 1906 to 1923. By 1925 they were no longer in demand as the ill-fated attempts to publish papers in Houston, Galveston, and San Antonio demonstrate. The one exception was *La Tribuna Italiana* (1913-1962), which for almost fifty years, kept alive the glories of Italian culture among the Italian residents of Texas, Oklahoma, and Louisiana.

La Tribuna Italiana survived longer than the other Texas-based Italian newspapers largely through the journalistic ability and determination of its founder, Car-

[21] Barker Historical Collection of Newspapers, University of Texas, Austin, Texas.

[22] *La Stella del Texas,* June 7, 1913, Rosenberg Archives, Galveston, Texas.

[23] *La Patria degli Italiani.* 1925. Rosenberg Archives, Galveston, Texas.

[24] *Houston City Directory* (1906-1925), Houston Public Library.

lo Saverio Papa. Papa, an immigrant from Cefalu, Sicily, came to the United States in 1904, and operated barbershops in Baltimore and Richmond until 1908. He came to Dallas in May of that year and managed a barbershop until he began publishing *La Tribuna Italiana*. Initially, Papa had no press, no printer, no staff, and little money. Then in 1916, Louis Adin, a printer of considerable experience, arrived from Italy by way of El Paso. Adin became a full partner in Papa's paper. He wrote editorials and news columns, operated the linotype machine, and translated, composed, and set type all in one process. When Benito Mussolini declared war on the Allies in 1940, Papa and Adin changed the name of the paper to *The Texas Tribune* and began publishing it entirely in English. When Papa died in 1947, Joseph Gennaro became the editor, and the paper continued to circulate until December, 1962.[25]

Benevolent-fraternal societies were also important to many urban Italians in Texas between 1880 and 1920. These societies were formed primarily to provide its members with sick benefits, funeral expenses, insurance, and social activities. *La Stella D'Italia*, established in Galveston in 1876, may have been the first Italian mutual aid society in Texas. Italians also formed the Garibaldi Odd Fellows Lodge at Galveston in 1884, and the organization acquired 100 members by the onset of World War I.[26] The oldest mutual aid society in Galveston with a charter on file with the Office of the Secretary of State is the *Societa Italiana Meridionale di Mutuo Soccorso*. This organization received its charter on August 17, 1909. The names of its directors were Gioacchino Cassara, Rosario Vassallo, Filippo Liberto, Giacomo Mancuso, Francesco Torregrossa, Michele Megna,

[25] Joseph P. Gennaro, private interview held at 15910 Coolwood Drive, Dallas, Texas, January 7, 1982.

[26] James O. Bailey, *Aspects of Italian Immigration Into Southeast Texas*. M.A. Thesis, University of Houston (Clear Lake City, 1977), p. 58.

Giuseppe N. Arena, and Pietro Fria.[27] The association had no capital stock and was formed "for benevolent and charitable purposes." On January 27, 1911, the directors of the organization changed its name to *Societa Italiana di Mutuo Soccorso Stella D'Italia.*

Before the turn of the century two Italian societies were also established in Houston. The first one was the Queen Marguerite Sovoia Benefit Society, which was formed in 1888 and had a membership of eighty-six people in 1893. The second one was the Christopher Columbus Mutual Benefit Association which was formed in 1897 and had a membership of eighty-five people during the first decade of its existence.[28] The oldest Italian mutual aid society in Texas with a charter on file with the Office of the Secretary of State is the *Societa Italiana di Mutuo Soccorso di San Antonio Texas,* founded in San Antonio on April 4, 1884. The names of its directors were: Antonio Bruni, Augustine Rubino, Francesco Rubiolo, Jose Cassiano, Luigi Moglia, and Paolo Columbo. The charter of the organization states that "This corporation is formed for the purpose of mutual relief among its members, social intercourse and union of Italian people and their descendants." [29] In 1890 Cavaliere Carlo Alberto Solaro and fifteen compatriots founded the Christopher Columbus Society of San Antonio. The organization was a combination of a benevolent society and a fraternal organization. In the early years it loaned money to needy Italian families, furnished advice and counsel in business matters, taught English to new arrivals, and provided a framework for social activities. From its beginning Italian was the official language of the society.

[27] Texas, Office of the Secretary of State, Charter of the Societa Italiana Meridionale di Mutuo Soccorso. Charter No. 20649. Austin, Texas, August 17, 1909.

[28] *Houston City Directory* (1888-1907), Houston Public Library.

[29] Texas, Office of the Secretary of State, Charter of the Societa Italiana di Mutuo Soccorso di San Antonio Texas. Charter No. 2354. Austin, Texas, April 21, 1884.

Then in 1946 the language was changed to English.[30]

Around 1890, the lumber business replaced flour and grist milling as the state's first-ranking industry. The pine forests of East Texas had long supplied a steady basis for the sawmills and planing mills developed during the period of the Republic. The production of pine lumber was focused at Orange and Beaumont, where in 1870 yearly production topped one hundred million board feet. The forests of East Texas covered an estimated 68,000 square miles and had a potential yield variously estimated to be between 70 and 300 billion board feet. Meanwhile, the fantastic production of oil at the turn of the century brought several developments besides enthusiastic speculation. Hundreds of companies were organized, some of which became giants in the field. Among these was the Gulf Oil Company, which was started in 1901 as the Guffey Oil Company with a refinery in Port Arthur.[31] Lumbering and the oil industry provided job opportunities for Italians who came to Jefferson and Orange counties to work in the sawmills and refineries located there. In 1920 there were 832 and 56 foreign-born Italians living in Jefferson and Orange Counties, respectively.[32]

Marion Aquilina was born in the village of Caltabellota, in the province of Agrigento, Sicily, on April 5,

[30] William Kelly, president, and Michele Rizzo, president emeritus, private interview held at the Christopher Columbus Italian Society, 201 Morales Street, San Antonio, Texas, August 14, 1981. The author conducted a thorough search among the manuscript holdings of the Barker Texas History Center in Austin; the Lorenzo de Zavala State Archives and Library Building in Austin; and the library of the Institute of Texan Cultures in San Antonio; for information about the Italian benevolent-fraternal societies in Texas. None of these institutions has any records of these societies.

[31] Seymour V. Connor, *Texas: A History.* (Arlington Heights, Illinois: AHM, 1971), pp. 272-273.

[32] United States Census Office, Fourteenth Census of the United States 1920, Volume III, Population, Washington, D.C., pp. 1022-1023.

1889. Aquilina came to Jefferson County in 1902 via New Orleans at the age of thirteen, and he worked in the sawmills for seven years. The young Italian managed to save enough money to buy a small grocery store in Port Arthur in 1909. In 1913 he married Angela Benedetto, and the couple had four children. Most of their time was spent operating the family store. The few diversions they allowed themselves included activities associated with St. Mary's Catholic Church and visits with friends. Marion invested in real estate and the family prospered. The eldest son, Sam Aquilina, was knighted by the Italian government in 1982 for his many civic contributions to Port Arthur. Sam Aquilina is an intelligent, charming gentleman with a captivating smile. His brown eyes beneath dark hair sparkle when he discusses the Italians of Jefferson County. According to him, "The Italians of Port Arthur seemed to manage very well in rearing and educating their families. They were hard-working, honest, religious people that I grew to admire and love. Their sons and daughters have also made fine citizens. They learned important lessons from the labors of their immigrant parents." [33]

In 1920 there were also 182 foreign-born Italians living in El Paso, Texas.[34] El Paso was a terminus of the Texas Pacific, the Atchison, Topeka & Santa Fe, the Mexican Central railroads and an important point on the Southern Pacific. The railroads brought industries to the city with the opening of their shops. In 1885, Robert Towne built the custom smelter of the American Smelting and Refining Company, the only lead plant in the Southwest. Other industries included flour milling, cement manufacturing, cotton milling, oil refining, making of optical instruments, brewing, cotton ginning, bottling, and meat packing.[35]

[33] Sam Aquilina, private interview held at 100 Eddington Court, Port Arthur, Texas, June 10, 1982.

[34] Fourteenth Census of the United States, *op. cit.*, p. 1022.

[35] Nancy I. Hammons, *A History of El Paso County.* (M.A. thesis, College of Mines, 1942), pp. 32-46.

Salvatore Piccolo was born in Trapani, Sicily, in 1875. In 1896 he married Giovanna Bonavita from that same city, and the couple moved to El Paso via New Orleans shortly thereafter. Salvatore found work as a laborer in the American Smelting and Refining Company. He performed backbreaking, tiresome tasks to help produce lead for lining tanks and tea chests, for the manufacture of lead pipe and for making many alloys and compounds. Giovanna took in sewing to add to the family income. In 1907 Salvatore opened a confectionery store, which afforded him, his wife, and their two children a comfortable life style. Salvatore's grandson, David Piccolo, is a successful attorney in Oklahoma City. He is a burly, bearded man with twinkling brown eyes and a beaming personality. On the day that I interviewed him, he was meticulously dressed. According to him, Italians went to El Paso County seeking bread and work. I asked him to account for their success in adapting and prospering in their new environment. He replied: "The Italians of El Paso County were hard-working, patient people. The men were firm, constant with their families, with their neighbors, and in all things. The women were serious and the cohesive force which bound the families together and thus provided a bedrock for the entire ethnic group." [36]

CONCLUSION

In proportion to their numbers, Italians played significant roles in the early urban life of Texas. These people adapted nonurban institutions from their native villages to the urban milieu in Texas in order to survive and prosper. But modern Italian Texans no longer need the support systems of their forebears, because they have adopted many of the sociocultural characteristics of the dominant culture. Italian neighborhoods in Texas cities have been fragmented by urban renewal, or decimated

---

[36] David Piccolo, private interview held at the Texas Woman's University, Denton, Texas, August 20, 1982.

by the suburban exodus. However, the family unit remains important to most of these people, and a majority of them still belong to the Catholic Church. Italians are proud of their heritage. They continue to prepare old family recipes, and many of them have made visits to relatives in Italy. The Italian language has largely fallen into disuse. Nevertheless, most Italian Americans are familiar with Italian terms and phrases, and some urban Italian clubs in Texas offer courses in the Italian language. In addition, among members of this ethnic group there is often an immediate, subliminal understanding, based upon shared values and attitudes, which is conveyed through body gestures and facial expressions. The benevolent-fraternal organizations have been replaced by Italian clubs which emphasize social, festive, and cultural events. These newer organizations commonly sponsor humanitarian projects. For example, when a series of earthquakes struck southern Italy in November, 1980, Italian organizations in Texas raised thousands of dollars in aid for the victims of that disaster.

ITALIAN MINERS
AND RAILROAD WORKERS

*Patria est ubicumque vir fortis sedem
sibi elegerit.*

*A brave man's country is wherever
he chooses to settle.* — *Q. Curtius
Rufus, Exploits of Alexander,* VI, iv, 11.

ITALIAN COAL MINERS

Midway between Fort Worth and Abilene, Texas, on Highway 80, stands an enormous red brick smokestack and three scattered buildings. They are all that remain of the once thriving town of Thurber. Here the Texas Pacific Coal Company recruited immigrants in the 1880s to work its rich coal mines. From 1888 until 1921, Thurber coal was preferred by railroad firemen, householders, and varied fuel users throughout a five-state area. The highly productive mines were the only source of commercial bituminous coal in Texas. For more than three decades shafts pierced the rolling hills around Thurber and yielded the hard, high-grade coal, which supported one of Texas' major industries of that time.[1] The mines supplied several thousand tons of coal every day. Workers dug shafts to the coal vein, removed earth from above and below the vein, and then dynamited. They erected tipples over each shaft to raise the coal to the surface.[2]

[1] William B. Alderman, "Seagram Builds an Oil Company," *Texas Parade.* Austin, Texas, July 1968, pp. 2-3.

[2] John H. Poerner (Chairman), *Historical Coal Mines in Texas: An Annotated Bibliography.* (Austin: Railroad Commission of Texas, Surface Mining and Reclamation Division, 1979), p. 9.

ITALIAN MINERS from the Texas and Pacific Coal Company in Thurber, Texas

— Courtesy Texas Pacific Oil Company, Dallas, Texas
Copy From U.T. Institute of Texan Cultures,
San Antonio, Texas

Thurber's second industry began in 1897, after it was discovered that the area contained rich deposits of shale clay, well suited for the manufacture of vitrified bricks. In 1918, the Thurber Brick Plant produced two million bricks per month. Thurber brick can be seen in the streets of Fort Worth and sea wall at Galveston.

Many employees were needed for work related to mining. Occupations included superintendents, managers, foremen, bookkeepers, cashiers, assistants, clerks, collectors, draftsmen, messengers, errand boys, and purchasing agents. There were also stenographers and typists, blacksmiths, boilermakers, carpenters, trackmen, stablemen, electricians, engineers, machinists, mill wrights, cutters, masons, mechanics, inspectors, and other laborers. The brick yards required special workmen, and some people were involved in community services. Thus in 1910 there were 2,500 miners out of a total population of about 7,000 persons living in Thurber.[3] More than 10,000 people lived in Thurber at its zenith. The miners represented about twenty different nationalities, mainly European, although Italians and Poles did most of the mining.[4] While searching the public records of Erath County, and the parish records of St. Rita's Catholic Church at Ranger, Texas, for the oldest document involving an Italian resident of Thurber, the author discovered a birth certificate for Bernardo Barra.[5] The child was born on December 8, 1892. He was the son of Costantino Barra, and Maddalena Brunetta. Bernardo Barra was baptized at St. James Catholic Church in Thurber. The church was built in 1892, and it was moved to Mingus in 1937.

Some of the mine workers reached Thurber by way

[3] *Report of the United States Coal Commission*, Volume III, (U.S. Government Printing Office, Washington, D.C., 1925), p. 1257.

[4] Institute of Texan Cultures, *The Italian Texans.* (San Antonio: University of Texas, 1973), p. 14.

[5] Texas, certificate of baptism issued January 29, 1893, recorded in St. Rita's Catholic Church, Ranger, Texas.

of the Pennsylvania fields, but most of them came directly from their homelands. The Texas Pacific Coal Company maintained employment offices in New York, New Orleans, and Galveston. Company officials attached a destination tag to the clothing of newly hired foreign employees, and then placed them on a train bound for Thurber. In most instances a man would work in the mines for several months before sending for his family. Many Italian workers came directly to Thurber on the advise of friends or relatives already working there.[6]

The company erected two schools before 1895 for Catholic immigrants. The schools were operated under the supervision of the Sisters of Incarnate Word, from San Antonio. These institutions provided night classes for boys, until they closed in 1923. Thurber's first school was established on the ground floor of the Knights of Labor hall. Thurber had numerous art and music teachers, and classes were conducted at various locations within the town. At one time, thurber had the only public library in Erath County.[7] The company employed a small staff of doctors and established a modest emergency hospital. Employees were hired with the understanding that a charge would be deducted each month from their earnings as insurance for medical and hospital care. The rate varied between fifty cents and one dollar a month. Physicians were hired and paid by the coal company. They were sanitation engineers as well as physicians in that their duties included the supervision of garbage and sewage disposal, water purification, and the assurance of general sanitary practices.

Many Italians were pleased with their lives in Texas. After 1893, hundreds of them applied to become naturalized American citizens. The following Italian surnames were picked at random from the records in the district

[6] Rico Beneventi, John Biondini, private interview held at Box 164, Mingus, Texas, February 7, 1981.

[7] Texas and Pacific Coal Company, Unpublished Company Records, Southwest Collection, Texas Tech University, Lubbock, Texas.

clerk's office at Stephenville: Beratti, Coppi, Ceredono, Donatti, Papperio, Favarrio, Camillo, and Rafelli.[8] Italians also mined copper, zinc, and lead in other parts of Texas.[9] The Hazel Copper-Silver Mine of Culberson County yielded about one million pounds of copper from 1891 to 1947, but all mines are now closed. Lead and zinc were extracted chiefly from the Presidio Mine in Presidio County and the Bird Mine in Brewster County, but these minerals have not been mined in Texas since 1952. In 1890 there were no Italians living in Erath County. By 1900, 429 of them had settled there, and by 1910 their numbers had increased to 729.[10] Then the Italian population of the county began to decline. Table VIII shows the number of foreign-born Italians living in Erath County between 1890 and 1940.

TABLE VIII. Foreign-Born Italians
Resident in Erath County: 1890-1940.

Year	No. of Italians
1890	none listed
1900	429
1910	729
1920	267
1930	6
1940	1

Sources: United States Census Office, Eleventh Census of the United States (1890), Population, Volume I, Part I, 1895, p. 661.

Twelfth Census of the United States (1900), Population, Part I, 1901, p. 784.

[8] Texas, Erath County, Naturalization, Petition and Record, Volume I; Record of Declaration of Intention, Volume I. (1892-1917).

[9] Andrew F. Rolle, *The Immigrant Upraised.* (Norman: University of Oklahoma Press, 1968), p. 228.

[10] Twelfth Census of the United States, 1900. Vol. I. Population, p. 784; Thirteenth Census of the United States, 1910, Vol. III. Population, p. 808.

Thirteenth Census of the United States (1910), Population, Volume III, 1913, p. 835.

Fourteenth Census of the United States (1920), Population, Volume III, 1922, p. 1022.

Fifteenth Census of the United States (1930), Population, Volume III, Part II, 1932, p. 1017.

Sixteenth Census of the United States (1940), Population, Volume II, Part VI, 1943, p. 899.

In 1905, foreign-born Italians were still arriving at Thurber. Eliot Lord reported ". . . about eight hundred miners of various nationalities were at work. More than one-third of these were Italians. The local Italian colony here numbers about five hundred, including women and children. Its workmen are for the greater part Venetians, Piedmontese and Modenese . . . the Italians were the best workmen . . . The Colony of Thurber . . . is as industrious and tranquil as anyone could desire. There are very few disturbances, as is evident from the fact that there is only one policeman in the town, who is able to maintain order throughout the town as well as in the surrounding area." [11] In his book, *The Italian in America,* Lord describes working conditions in the mines. "The mines are located from three to six miles from the village, but in the morning and evening the miners are taken to work and back to their homes by two special trains. It was stated by the Italian workers at Thurber that the mining was hard because the stratum of coal was thin and the galleries therefore low, so that it was necessary to work in a crouching position; but, on the other hand, there was assurance of safety from the fact that the coal did not give off gas and that the galleries were perfectly dry. In consequence of the intervention of the United Mine Workers of America, it was said that from the 1st of October of the year, 1903, the working day had been reduced to eight hours and the pay in-

[11] Eliot Lord, *The Italian in America.* (New York: B.F. Buck, 1905), pp. 110-112.

creased to $1.17 ½ per ton. A delegate of the union now assists at the weighing of coal in every mine." [12]

Italians were quite active in union affairs. Joe Pogiani administered the financial transactions of the local chapter of the United Mine Workers at Thurber, and another Italian with the surname Pasconi, served as the last officer of Italian local No. 2763. During the regular and special sessions of the Texas state legislature of 1921, "Joe Americus, a capable young Italian, was lobbying at Austin as business agent for the Union." [13] The union proved to be a boon to the coal miners. Lord states that, "All the miners work by the piece, and according to their greater or lesser ability are earning from $2.50 to $3.00 and sometimes more per day. Inexperienced workers, on arrival, who begin as apprentices, earn at the start 1.00 per day, but in a few weeks they are said to learn the work and their wages increase week by week . . . needed food supplies, bread, meat, fish, etc., are cheap. The unmarried miners are accustomed to live in boarding houses with families either of relatives or fellow-countrymen, paying for board $16.00 per month. The greater part, . . . make notable savings; very few indeed spend all of their wages." [14] When the miners had accumulated a few hundred dollars, they mailed their savings to banks in Italy. Some skeptical Italians did not trust banks, and preferred to bury their money in jars until they had enough to send overseas. From time to time some individuals left Thurber for visits to Italy.

Poles and Italians lived on Hill Number 3 of Thurber. A railroad track to the mines bisected the hill, with the Poles residing on the south side and the Italians on the north. A report issued by the Thurber Historical Association states that the Italian miners were "unques-

[12] *Ibid.*, p. 112.
[13] Lorenzo Santi, private interview held at Mingus, Texas, August 11, 1967 by Nancy Spoede. Tape in possession of the Southwest Collection, Texas Tech University, Lubbock, Texas.
[14] Lord, *The Italian in America*, op. cit., pp. 112-113.

tionably Thurber's most colorful citizens." [15] But they were clannish to the point of dividing within groups according to their places of origin in Italy. Italians love music of all kinds. During its heyday Thurber had an opera house which was well attended by many enthusiastic Italian patrons. It could accommodate 655 people, and its thirty by fifty-foot stage was lighted by electric lamps. The opera house hosted its first opera in 1896, and from then on Thurber was visited by opera companies between their stops at Fort Worth and El Paso. Many Italians were somewhat artistic, and had beautiful voices, and these people participated in operatic performances. *Il Trovatore* (the troubadour) was a favorite opera at Thurber, as were many of Giuseppe Verdi's compositions. But musical tastes were not limited to opera. The community at Thurber produced an excellent band which often played at the Dallas Fair. In addition, on almost any evening one could enjoy the melodic sounds of an accordionist as he sat in the doorway of his home playing Italian folk songs. He rarely played alone for very long, because there were usually others eager to accompany him on mandolins, flutes, and violins, or merely to sing. Neighbors would walk out into their yards or sit on their doorsteps to listen.

At Thurber, the Fourth of July, Labor Day, and assorted European holidays were occasions for lavish celebrations. Regardless of nationality, people would turn out to honor the holiday queen, participate in sporting events, and dance to the music of Mexican, American, and Italian bands.[16] Most families had homes with an outside oven and cellar. The more elaborate cellars had coolers to accommodate the storage of cheese and meats. Italians ordered carloads of grapes from California in order to make *vino* (wine) and *grappa* (brandy). Wine cellars were usually walled and floored with brick. Dur-

[15] Lamar Haines, *A Pictorial Souvenir of Early Thurber Days.* (Stephenville: Thurber Historical Society, 1966), p. 10.
[16] *Ibid.,* p. 6.

THE SEVENTH FLAG OVER TEXAS. Italian miners unfurl the Italian flag at a club picnic. Thurber, Texas, 1890.

— Courtesy Texas Pacific Oil Company, Dallas, Texas.
Copy From U.T. Institute of Texan Cultures,
San Antonio, Texas

ing the prohibition era much of the wine consumed was made in these cellars.[17] In Italian homes with boarders, there was usually a large icebox built on one side of the house. This was called the "beer icebox." Sometimes friends would come over for a drink, and when they emptied a keg, they would contribute towards the cost. On Sunday afternoons during warm weather, the men would sometimes drink several kegs of beer. But meals were almost always accompanied by wine.

Food was a featured attraction at the elaborate Italian weddings. Women served a rice dish called *risotto*, with salads, various kinds of meats, homemade bread, and barrels of wine. They cooked the rice in large black pots, into which went gallons of chicken broth, giblets, tomato sauce, and grated cheese. *Pane fresco e vino vecchio* (fresh bread and old wine) went together in the minds of many Italian miners. Each Italian home had its back yard oven where homemade bread was baked. A fire would be lighted in the oven and allowed to burn until the bricks reached the desired temperature for baking. The fire was then removed and the loaves placed in the oven by means of a long-handled wooden shovel and allowed to bake until done. This bread had a heavier texture and thicker crust than American bread and was preferred by Italians over the bread baked in the company bakery. Bread was baked twice weekly and on baking days an appetizing aroma of fresh-baked bread permeated the entire community.[18] Pork products were universally popular with the Italians of Thurber. Unlike cattle and sheep, which are raised only in some parts of Italy, pigs fare well — in fact, prosper — all over the country. During wintertime in Thurber, Italian families slaughtered their hogs, and everyone including the boarders, helped with the cutting and grinding. Wives prepared

[17] Lorenzo Santi, private interview held at the Blalock Nursing Home, 8955 Long Point, Houston, Texas, January 30, 1981.

[18] Geno Solignani, private interview held at Box 164, Mingus, Texas, February 7, 1981.

cotechino (cooking salami) and *guanciale* (unsmoked bacon) from lean hog meat. They also made *prosciutto* (cured, unsmoked ham), *mortadella* (the original bologna), and cooked the liver, the rind, the feet, and the knuckles. Pigs' feet and knuckles were particularly popular with the northern Italians, especially as winter dishes.

Festivals and weddings must have been delightful events. Men and women dressed in varied costumes of blue, green, and purple. The Italians had their own dance hall, where they danced to native and American music. On Italian holidays, women characteristically wore brightly colored ribbons attached to their belts, and had lovely silver ornaments for head decorations. Men wore rather wide-brimmed hats and sleeveless vests. Both sexes wore white knitted stockings and homemade black slippers. There was much room for flirtation during folk dancing. As the wine kegs were emptied they were stacked atop each other. The success of the festivity was measured by the height of the pyramid.[19] *Bocce* was also a favorite form of diversion. A miniature Mardi Gras-type celebration marked the eve of the Lenten season. Men dressed in colorful costumes went house-to-house, entertaining children. At each home the mother served *crostata* (a small pastry containing plum or cherry jam), coffee, and wine. The homemade wine was sometimes a problem for federal agents who were trying to enforce the national prohibition which began on January 29, 1919. If there was sufficient advance warning, the Italians moved the wine to secret hiding places. Otherwise, the kegs were quickly poured on the ground. When law enforcement personnel arrived, the houses were empty of alcoholic beverages and no one knew anything about the aromatic rivulets trickling down the hillside.

Of all the Italians who settled at Thurber during its coal mining era, no name looms larger than that of Lorenzo Santi. Santi was born at Pievepelago, Modena,

[19] Institute of Texan Cultures, *The Italian Texans, op. cit.,* p. 14.

JOSEPH and ADA TELFENER with their children in Rome, 1887.

Emilia-Romagna, on August 2, 1893. He came to America in January 1911, and settled at Thurber on September 1, 1913. Santi worked in the mines, became a naturalized citizen of the United States about 1930, and was very active in the United Mine Workers of America. He attended several national conventions of this organization, and also served as a delegate to national and state meetings of the American Federation of Labor. Santi was regional director of the United Mine Workers: an area that included Texas, Arkansas, and Oklahoma. He later became a prominent businessman engaged in general merchandising,[20] and was elected mayor of the city of Mingus, serving in that office for twenty-six years. During an exclusive interview held at the Blalock Nursing Home, Houston, Texas, on January 30, 1981, the author asked Mr. Santi to mention the major contributions of Italians to Texas during the first two decades of this century. He explained that "The Italians worked very hard in the mines at Thurber, and thereby, helped to provide an important fuel used at that time by many Texas homes and industries . . . Italians also played important roles in the local chapter of the United Mine Workers." [21]

In 1918 oil strikes in the nearby Ranger field marked the beginning of the end of Thurber as a mining town, since oil was a cheaper source of energy than coal. But an examination of the payroll ledger for the Texas Pacific Coal and Oil Company, demonstrates that in January 1920 scores of men with Italian surnames were still working in the mines.[22] A few examples include: Ambrozio Tillano, Jack Gambotti, Constantino Santi, James Gardetto, Pete Colombotto, Nick Reginatto, and Ercoli Carrari. Most of the mines closed in 1921, and Italian

[20] For an excellent presentation of the history of organized labor in Texas, consult — Ruth Allen, *Chapters in the History of Organized Labor in Texas.* (Austin: University of Texas Press, 1941).

[21] Lorenzo Santi, private interview, January 30, 1981. *op. cit.*

[22] The payroll ledger is in the possession of Geno Solignani, Box 164, Mingus, Texas.

laborers scattered to nearby towns, went to other parts of the country, or returned to their homelands. A few Italians established homes in the southwest part of Palo Pinto County. They picked pecans, secured small farms, worked on road construction, or found other kinds of employment. Between 1910 and 1920, the number of Italians decreased from 729 to 267 in Erath County, but increased from 79 to 159 in Palo Pinto County.[23] Descendants of these miners still live in Mingus and Strawn.

Luigi Solignani, his wife Beatricia Rossi, and their three children moved to Mingus after the mines closed. Luigi and Beatricia were born near Modena, and were married in that province. They moved to Thurber with their daughter Olympia *via* New York in 1905. Luigi worked in the mines and the family worshipped at St. James Catholic Church. But Beatricia died in 1921 when a flu epidemic swept the city. Luigi became active in a fraternal and benevolent society known as *stella d'italia.* The organization sponsored various social functions and did charitable work for orphanages and the community at large.[24] When the coal mines completely closed down, clusters of emotional Italians embraced one another, tears flowing as they said their farewells. "Some prayed that the saints would watch over their Thurber friends." Official U.S. Census records indicate that there were six foreign-born Italians living in Erath County in 1930, and ten years later there was only one native Italian in the entire county.[25] Today, Thurber is a ghost town.

---

[23] Fourteenth Census of the United States, 1920, Vol. III, p. 1022; Texas, Palo Pinto County, "Reverse Index to Deeds," "General Index to Deeds," Volumes E-Z, Volumes 1-114 (1880-1920).

[24] Geno Solignani, private interview, February 7, 1981, *op. cit.*

[25] Fourteenth Census of the United States, 1920, Vol. III, Population, p. 1022; Fifteenth Census of the United States, 1930, Vol. III, Part 2, Population, p. 1016; Sixteenth Census of the United States, 1940, Vol. II, Part 6, Population, p. 897.

ITALIAN RAILROAD WORKERS

On July 4, 1882, on the one hundred and sixth anniversary of the United States, the remnants of a group of 1,200 Italian laborers, mostly from the region of Lombardy, completed the construction of ninety-one miles of railroad tracks from Victoria to Rosenberg, Texas. Count Giuseppe Telfener directed the building of the railroad at a cost of two million dollars. Very little is known about the early life of Count Telfener. In the *Enciclopedia Storico Nobiliare Italiana,* Rome is indicated as the *dimora* (residence) of the family. In the *Albo Nazionale Famiglie Nobili Italiene,* the Telfeners are listed as a "famiglia fiorentina di origine austriaca" (a Florentine family of Austrian origin). Upon the author's request, Paolo Bonfi, director of the Florence State Archives, initiated an unsuccessful search for Count Telfener's birth certificate. Mr. Bonfi explained by letter that there were two possible reasons why the document is not among the holdings of the state archives. Either the count was not Catholic, or he was not born in Florence or anywhere else in Tuscany.[26] The Valuation Report of the Galveston, Harrisburg and San Antonio Railway as of June 30, 1918, states that Telfener was from Rome, Italy.[27] When nobled by King Victor Emmanuel II in 1877, Giuseppe Telfener was a millionaire, and the owner of Villa Potenziani and other palaces in Rome.[28] Many Italian races of that time were won by Telfener horses. Telfener owned several racing stables in Italy, one of which had 200 horses.[29]

[26] Vittorio Spreti, *Enciclopedia Storico-Nobiliare Italiana,* Roma, 1907, Vol. VI, p. 567; *Albo Nazionale Famiglie Nobili Italiene,* (Via Verga 4, Milano, 1911), p. 484; Railroad Commission of Texas, Transportation Division, Valuation Report of the Galveston, Harrisburg and San Antonio Railway as of June 30, 1918, Austin, Texas, p. 38.

[27] Letter fron Paolo Bonfi, director, Florence State Archives, Florence, Italy, June 2, 1982.

[28] Giovanni Schiavo, *Four Centuries of Italian-American History.* (New York: Vigo, 1955), p. 310.

[29] "An Italian Railroad King," *South American Journal and Brazil and River Plate Mail,* July 5, 1883.

COUNT JOSEPH TELFENER (center, seated) and the directors of the Macaroni Line of the
N.Y. Texan & Mexican Railroad Co. 1881.

— Courtesy Frank E. Tritico, Houston, Texas
Copy From U.T. Institute of Texan Cultures,
San Antonio, Texas

The railroad that Telfener built had an interesting inception. J. W. Mackay, a mining millionaire of the 1870s and his wife, met Telfener while traveling in Europe. The count had just completed a 350-mile rail line between Cordova and Tucuman for the government of Argentina.[30] The two men discussed the possibilities of building railways in Texas. Telfener conceived a plan of bringing Italian workmen to Texas, who would later settle on lands which at that time could be secured by state grants for railroad construction. On March 15, 1879, Telfener married an American, Ada Hungerford, in Rome at Palazzo Telfener, formerly a royal residence. The king of Italy, and Monsignore Cataldi, a representative of the Pope, attended the wedding. Giuseppe and Ada parented four children.

In 1880, Telfener, his father-in-law Colonel Daniel E. Hungerford, Mackay and several European, New York, and Texas financiers, developed a plan to link New York and Mexico by rail. They and others signed the New York, Texas, and Mexican Railway Company charter on October 18, 1880, in Paris, France, and filed the document in Austin, Texas, on November 17. Among those who formed the corporation with Telfener was Giovanni Della Spina of Rome. Spina became one of the first board of directors of the company.[31] The corporate directors chose Texas as the starting point for the railroad because the state offered sixteen sections of land (10,240 acres), for each mile of track completed. The builders readily arranged to float bonds backed by land grants.

On November 17, Telfener secured a charter for a road to Brownsville. Richmond was to be the starting point but this was later changed to Rosenberg. The route was through Victoria with branches to Lavaca Bay and

[30] "The New York, Texas and Mexican Railway Company," *South American Journal and Brazil and River Plate Mail,* April 27, 1882.

[31] Article of Association for the Incorporation of the New York, Texas, and Mexican Railway Company, 1880. Railroad Charters and Amendments. (Secretary of State, Austin), Book A, 250.

Corpus Christi. Meanwhile, the count formulated plans for building a line from Brownsville into Mexico.[32] Telfener signed a contract with the company dated June 16, 1881, for work which began west from Rosenberg Junction and east from Victoria in September. The daily wages for the imported workers ranged from $1.50 for common labor up to $4.00 for some skilled tasks. Telfener paid for the workers' trips from Italy to Texas. He also supplied them with food, clothing, and shelter until they began earning wages. The count even offered to partially finance the journeys of the workers' families to Texas, after completion of the project. Telfener hoped that these people would become American citizens, and that they would settle along the railroad line. If his plan worked, the Italian families would help to provide business for the railroad.[33]

Workmen used crude tools and primitive methods to construct the line. Because they did not have a pile driver during the early stages of the work, it required twelve laborers to drive piles for the bridges by means of a rope threaded pulley. The pulley raised a huge live oak block high into the air. When tripped it slammed down upon the pile heads with a resounding thump to give the necessary penetration. Rain and resistant heavy black soil delayed the laying of track west of Wharton. As soon as construction crews threw up earth for the roadbed, rain washed it down again. To solve this Sisyphean problem, the workers laid brush and small trees and other debris along the roadbed, and placed red clay upon them. Teams of horses were useless in the miry mass along the right-of-way, and workmen used hand cars to transport rails and ties to the construction sites.[34]

[32] S. G. Reed, *A History of the Texas Railroads.* (Houston: St. Clair, 1941), pp. 264-265.

[33] "Run Over the Telfener Railroad," *Galveston News,* March 31, 1882; "The New York, Texas, and Mexican Railroad and Its Italian Laborers," *Galveston News,* April 1, 1882.

[34] S. G. Reed, "High Railroad Officials Get Training Here," *Victoria Advocate,* September 28, 1934, sect. 13, p. 101; John C. Ray-

Official U.S. Census records indicate that there were no Italians living in Victoria County prior to the construction of the railroad. But in 1890, fifty-six foreign-born Italians resided in the county.[35] Research by the author at the Victoria County Historical Commission, and the Victoria Public Library, Victoria, Texas, yielded very little information about the Italian workers. The *Victoria Sesquicentennial Scrapbook: 1824-1974,* lists the following Italian names: Conti, Rippamonti, Tibiletti, Chiodini, Bianchi, Tagliabue, Santino Magnia, Vanelli, Rossi, Castelli, Pessini, Coati, Jim Sala, Riggamonti, Jasper Fossati, Miori, and Jim Zambelli.[36] The author examined the records of the Southern Pacific Transportation Company in Houston, Texas, for information about the Victoria-Rosenberg line. He discovered that what remains there pertains mostly to the twentieth century. Still, it was possible to obtain a copy of a page of the June 1882 payroll of the New York, Texas and Mexican Railway from Mr. Henry Hauschild, of Victoria, Texas. The document contains the names of forty-two Italian laborers.[37] (see appendix).

The descendants of many of these people live in Victoria, but most of them know very little about their Italian progenitors. However, by interviewing several senior citizens with Italian surnames, some of whom had family trees written into their Bibles, it was possible to glean some important information about the Italian railroad workers. Most of the immigrants appear to have been ten-

burn, "Count Joseph Telfener and the New York, Texas, and Mexican Railway Company," *Southwestern Historical Quarterly.* Vol. 68, July 1964-April 1965, p. 36.

[35] Tenth Census of the United States, 1880, Population, p. 530; Eleventh Census of the United States, 1890, Population, Vol. I, Part I, p. 663.

[36] *Victoria Sesquicentennial Scrapbook: 1824-1974.* (Victoria: Sears, 1975), p. 19.

[37] June, 1882, payroll of the New York, Texas and Mexican Railway. This document is in the possession of Henry Hauschild, 401 West Brazos, Victoria, Texas.

ITALIANS who worked on the N.Y., Texas & Mexican Railroad.
Clockwise from top center: Ignarzo Toss, Giacomo Zandonatti, Gia-
como Zambelli, Antonio Bartoni, Massimo Tasin, and Eugenio Depine
— *Courtesy Mr. & Mrs. Charles Innocenti.*
Copy From U.T. Institute of Texan Cultures,

ant farmers who earned bare subsistence wages in their native *comuni* (communities) in Italy. Some of these people came from Albizzate and Sumerago (Varese), Oregi (Milan), and Coccaglio (Brescia). All of these *comuni* and *provincie* (provinces) are in Lombardy. The voyage from Genoa to Galveston took forty-eight days. Men traveled without their families, and they began working on the railroad almost immediately upon their arrival at the construction sites. After railroad construction ended, those families who chose to remain in Victoria, returned to farming, or worked as laborers. City dwellers supplemented their incomes by taking in boarders and by growing vegetables in the back yard. The Italians of Victoria helped to build St. Mary's Catholic Church, and some of these people achieved prominent positions. For example, Mr. C. J. Fossati served two terms as city alderman. According to Mrs. F. X. Rippamonti, ". . . the Italians should be given credit for what they did to settle this country as they are wonderful and deserving people." [38]

The 88th Anniversary Number of the *Victoria Advocate* (1934) contains an article which mentions a few of the original immigrant workers. Among them is Jasper Fossati from Milan, Italy, who was Count Telfener's labor agent. Fossati is described as having been tall and thin. He married an opera singer, and was a good business man. Fossati entered the cattle business in DeWitt County and the venture proved to be a great success. He later sold his business and returned to Italy where he became a wealthy banker. A large number of men who came to Texas with the construction crews remained in the state and became solid, successful citizens. "Without any kind of government aid or special treatment they made their own way." [39] The staple food for these work-

[38] Private interviews with: Mrs. Francis Xavier Rippamonti, 1307 East Power Street, Victoria, Texas, April 27, 1982; Grace E. Rigamenti, 1906 East Red River Street, Victoria, Texas, May 18, 1982; Mrs. Annette Fossati, 406 Wagner Street, Victoria, Texas, May 24, 1982.

[39] Sidney R. Weisiger, "The Macaroni Railroaders," Anniversary Number of the *Victoria Advocate*. 18461934, p. 14.

ers was pasta shipped from Italy in wooden boxes, packed twenty and forty pounds to the container. The empty boxes were knocked apart and the boards used to build shanties in which the men could live.

Fossati's Restaurant and Delicatessen is the oldest business in Victoria. Francesco Fossati, an Italian immigrant from Brescia (Lombardy), founded the business in 1882. As a youth, he apprenticed as a stonecutter and spent ten years in Austria learning the fine points of the trade. In 1880, he came to New York. He learned from his friends that expert stonecutters were needed in Austin to help build a new state capitol. Fossati traveled to Austin, only to learn that the project was still in the planning stage. He found work as a laborer with the Southern Pacific Railroad, and helped to build the high bridge across the Pecos River in West Texas. Fossati then obtained a position in Victoria, cutting stone for a wage of three dollars a day. On March 1, 1882, he opened a chili and sandwich stand on Market Square. Fossati also sold imported cheeses, sausages, and olive oil. Gradually his business grew, and *Fossati's Delicatessen* became a popular meeting place for the Italians of Victoria, especially new arrivals.[40]

On March 18, 1882, the *Victoria Advocate* reported that a large number of Italian laborers were at work near the depot of the Gulf, Western Texas, and Pacific Railway, preparing a new bed for the ties and rails.[41] But rain and unfavorable working conditions caused widespread sickness among the work crews. Of the original 1,200 Italians brought to Texas by Telfener, only 600 remained on the job. The others had quit and drifted to various cities in the area. Because of his widely diversified financial interests, Telfener was in Texas for only short periods of time during the construction of the Texas line. He maintained an office in New York at the Nevada Bank on Wall Street. While in New York the count received hom-

---

[40] Institute of Texan Cultures, *The Italian Texans, op. cit.*, p. 31.
[41] "Railroad Notes," *Galveston News*, March 18, 1882.

age from members of the local Italian community, particularly Consul-General Raffo, and Vice-Consul Revel.[42]

By April 22, 1882, Texas had issued certificates for eight million acres of land more than was available for distribution, and so the state repealed all land grants to railroad builders. Construction on Telfener's railway stopped in July, but an excursion to Victoria from Houston formally opened for business on October 1. Telfener operated the railroad until July 23, 1884, and then he sold it to his brother-in-law, John W. Mackay on January 9, 1885. Mackay then sold the railroad to the Southern Pacific Lines in September of that year. Count Telfener continued to pursue his many financial interests, and he remained prosperous until his death in Rome on January 1, 1898. The town of Telfener is named in honor of Giuseppe Telfener. Descendants of the Italian railroad workers now live in Houston, Galveston, Victoria, and elsewhere in the state.[43]

Antonio Ghio was another Italian who was helpful to the Texas railroad industry. Ghio was born in Genoa (Liguria), Italy, in 1832, and he moved to New York in 1849. While in New York in 1862, Ghio married, and the couple had eight children. The family relocated to Jefferson, Texas, where they operated a successful mercantile store. But in the 1870s, the residents of Jefferson refused to allow railroad construction through their town. Ghio had strongly promoted the enterprise, and foresaw the decline of the town as a result of the obstinacy of its people. In 1873, he moved his family to Texarkana, and achieved great success there as a town builder. Ghio organized a Catholic Church, and worked for the achievement of advanced parochial education. In 1877 he and a partner built a brick opera house. Ghio then opened another theater in 1884, and three years later inaugurated Spring Lake Park. He also built an artificial gas

---

[42] Rayburn, "Count Joseph Telfener and the New York, Texas, and Mexican Railway Company," *op. cit.*, p. 33.

[43] Institute of Texan Cultures, *The Italian Texans, op. cit.*, p. 15.

plant and brought the first railroad to that part of the state. In 1880, the people of Texarkana elected him as their mayor. He served three terms in that office, and subsequently as alderman from his ward.[44]

CONCLUSION

Between 1880 and 1920, northern Italians came to Texas and sojourned or settled in the state. They mined coal, and helped to provide an important fuel used at that time by many Texas homes and industries. Men from Italy also worked to construct part of the great railroad network that underlaid the development of the sprawling state. They also played leading roles in the Thurber chapter of the United Mine Workers, and thereby, assisted miners to protect and promote their interests.

[44] Eugene C. Barker and F. J. Johnson, *Texas and Texans.* **Vol. V.** (American Historical Society, 1929), pp. 178-180.

ITALIAN FARM WORKERS
IN TEXAS

This is the farmer sowing his corn,
That kept the cock that crowed in the morn,
That milked the cow with the
crumpled horn — Nurse Truelove's
New Year's Gift (1755)

In the 1870s, the Italian immigration into Texas began to substantially increase. Immigrants from the *Mezzogiorno,* especially Sicily, settled primarily in the lower Brazos Valley and on the Galveston County mainland. Meanwhile, a few families from *Alta Italia* established farms in Montague County, and there were minor rural settlements elsewhere in Texas. But Italian farmers from Sicily spent gruelling months cutting sugar cane in southeast Louisiana, before coming to Texas to plant corn and cotton.

THE LOUISIANA CONNECTION

After the American Civil War, Louisiana and the other southern states were confronted with serious labor shortages due to the abolition of slavery and the migration of blacks to the North. The agricultural leaders of Louisiana decided to invite immigrant laborers to work in their sugar plantations. In 1866 Louisiana officials created the Bureau of Immigration to distribute pamphlets describing the resources of the state.[1] But this initial attempt met with only limited success. In 1870

[1] Louisiana, *Immigration Act, Statutes* (1866), Vol. III, pp. 1671-1678.

MEN LOADING strawberries on the "Katy Flyer" April 25, 1909. Dickinson, Texas.
— Photo by Frank Schlueter. From Beulah Owens Hughes.
Copy From U.T. Institute of Texan Cultures,

there were 1,884 Italians living in Louisiana. Approximately ninety-seven percent of these people were Sicilians. They had come from the north, central, and western sections of Sicily. Those who had emigrated directly, followed the citrus trade routes from Palermo and Messina to New Orleans.[2]

In July 1880 the bureau sent an experienced agent to Europe, and he succeeded in contracting several hundred agricultural workers. The Louisiana Sugar Planters' Association agreed to pay all of the necessary travel and living expenses of the new immigrants.[3] Of all the nationalities, the association preferred Italians because "they were said to be hard-working, thrifty, and content with few comforts."[4] To encourage the immigration of Italians to Louisiana, the Bureau of Immigration, in cooperation with the steamship lines that served New Orleans, established direct passage from Trieste, Palermo, and Naples.[5] With this accomplished the number of Italians emigrating to Louisiana began to grow. Of the 3,878 immigrants who arrived there in 1890, 2,611 came from Italy. Most ships bringing Italian immigrants and prod-

[2] Compendium of the Ninth Census of the United States (Washington, 1872), pp. 340-341; Guido Rossati and R. Enotenico, "Gl'Italiani nell' Agricoltura degli Stati Uniti D'America," in *Gli Italiani Negli Stati D'America*. (New York: Italian American Directory Company, 1906), p. 37; Italia, Ministero Degli Affari Esteri, Commissariato Generale Dell'Emigrazione, *Emigrazione E Colonie: Raccolta Di Rapporti Dell R. R. Agenti Diplomatici E Consolari*, Vol. III, *America* (Roma, 1909), pp. 202-221.

[3] Louisiana, Board of Agriculture and Immigration, *First Biennial Report of the Commission of Agriculture and Immigration for the years 1882-1883*. (Baton Rouge: Official Journal, 1884), p. 12; New Iberia *Louisiana Sugar Bowl*, February 24, 1881. This weekly newspaper focused primarily on matters of interest to sugar planters.

[4] J. Carlyle Sitterson,. *Sugar Country: The Cane Sugar Industry in the south, 1753-1950*. (Lexington, 1953), p. 315.

[5] Louisiana, Board of Agriculture and Immigration, *Fifteenth Biennial Report of the Commission of Agriculture and Immigration for the years 1910-1911*. (Baton Rouge: The New Advocate Official Journal, 1912), p. 14.

ucts to New Orleans during the late nineteenth century operated out of Palermo.

The *S.S. Po* which embarked from Palermo, Sicily, and arrived in New Orleans on December 8, 1891, was one of the many immigrant ships carrying a capacity load of 800-900 passengers, who would make the United States their home. Italians brought few resources with them. Seventeen dollars was the average, and many had nothing. The immigrants were crowded into steerage for the crossing which took several months. Frequently families would separate, sending one or two persons ahead to find work, and establish a residence; then other members of the family would join them. Italians did come to Louisiana but most did not stay. For the plantation worker too sought his dream in the expanding industrial and urban areas of the North. Meanwhile, Texas agricultural leaders were also faced with labor shortages in their corn and cotton fields. They offered generous sharecropping terms to entice European immigrants to come to their state, and many Italians responded by moving to Texas.[6]

BRAZOS VALLEY ITALIANS

Italians came to Texas between 1880 and 1914 primarily to improve their standards of living. Many of them wanted an opportunity to buy their own farms. The great extent of the state, the quality of the land, the climate, and the fact that Texas was somewhat closer than California to the large Eastern markets were all influencing factors. Italians began arriving in the lower Brazos Valley in the early 1870s, when a few families settled near Bryan. While searching the public records of

---

[6] Abstract of the Eleventh Census of the United States (Washington, 1894), pp. 38-39; U.S. Bureau of Customs, "Copies of Lists of Passengers Arriving in the Port of New Orleans, 1872-1894," National Archives Microcopy 382, Roll 2 (National Archives and Records Service); *Daily Picayune* (New Orleans), December 8, 1891, p. 2.

the office of the district clerk of Brazos County, for the oldest document involving an Italian, the author discovered a license for the marriage of Antonio Saladino and Bechin Mirri dated January 2, 1874.[7]

Businessmen in the Bryan area had long advertised in European newspapers for immigrants to come and help revitalize the local economy. Immigration was facilitated by the advance of the railroad through Brazos County in 1867-1869. In addition, the citizens of the county built an immigration house in Bryan for the convenience of newly arrived prospective settlers. They were allowed to live there free until they could find employment and living quarters.[8] The earliest Italians founded the Agricultural Benevolence Society, with J. M. Saladino as its first president. The society helped other newly arrived immigrants to make the necessary adjustments to their new environment.[9]

Italians did not begin arriving in Brazos County in large numbers until about 1880. They came primarily from three small farming communities in Sicily named Poggioreale, Corleone and Salaparuta.[10] These Italians had first settled in Louisiana where they cut sugar cane and accumulated some savings. Families made the important decision to move from Louisiana to the Brazos Valley because of the opportunity to buy their own land. They sailed to Houston from New Orleans and traveled to Bryan by train. 2,400 Sicilians who had worked as section

---

[7] Texas, marriage license issued January 2, 1874, recorded in Brazos County, Office of the District Clerk, Bryan, Texas.

[8] Elmer Grady Marshall, The History of Brazos County, Texas, M.A. Thesis, The University of Texas, Austin, August 1937, pp. 108-110.

[9] Lois Alyne Wilcox, The Early History of Bryan, Texas, M.A. Thesis, University of Texas, Austin, August 1952, pp. 81-82.

[10] James, Mary, and Marion J. Scarmardo, private interview held at 906 Mitchell Street, Bryan, Texas, June 22, 1980, Mary E. Dorsey, *Those Were The Days: Brazos County 1821-1921.* (Bryan: Fuller, 1976), p. 55.

hands on the Houston and Texas railroad, moved to Bryan after their labor was no longer needed on that project.[11]

The type of immigration that developed is known as district chain migration. The pattern for this type of immigration to Texas was established very early and was maintained throughout the period 1880 to 1920. The type of ethnic associations established by these people were largely derivative of the district chain migration type and the Italian settlement patterns. People from the Italian villages settled together in mixed rural Texas communities scattered over Brazos, Falls, Burleson, and Robertson counties. Take a pencil and a Texas map and draw lines connecting Bryan and Hearne and Caldwell. Within that triangle lies an area settled largely by Italian immigrants. Dilly Shaw, today situated north of Highway 21 and east of Highway 6, was part of a broad area in and around a plantation called Cameron Ranch. Many Italians settled there. The settlements were virtually self-contained and semi-isolated from other, similar, settlements. Consequently, these Sicilians first established local societies with membership based either on nationality or nationality/religion. The Agricultural Benevolence Society, parish organizations, and clubs established to promote local schools are all examples of the developing ethnicity of these people. The membership of Bryan's St. Anthony Catholic Church, founded by Italians in 1896, today has 651 families of Italian descent, representing two-thirds of the total membership.

At first the new settlers worked as sharecroppers and grew corn, cotton, and other crops in order to make enough money to buy farms and businesses. According to Johnny Lampo, a lifelong resident of Bryan, whose grandfather was one of the original Italian settlers, "The Italians proved that they could, on their own, establish their independence through farming, industry and private enterprise. They never looked for government hand-

[11] Andrew F. Rolle, *The Immigrant Upraised.* (Norman: University of Oklahoma Press, 1968), p. 226.

outs." [12] Johnny's father, Sam Lampo, said that one of the reasons for the success of the Italian people was their willingness to adapt. He indicated that a second reason was their custom of helping one another through the Benevolence Society: a custom that they had learned in Italy. "The Italian community was all one family. If a man who had started a crop became ill, we would all pitch in to harvest and sell his corn and cotton. We rendered this service free of charge. When a man lost his mule, the next morning he had another one on his lot. If a family became sick they were fed and cared for by other members of the community." [13]

The experiences of Giovanni Lampo, Sam Lampo's father, are rather typical of the many Italians who came to Bryan from Sicily. His brothers-in-law had found work in Louisiana and had urged him to join them. Giovanni arrived in New Orleans in 1874, and worked in the Louisiana cane fields for fifty cents a day. Nights he earned an extra twenty-five cents working in a sugar mill. Nine years after his arrival, Giovanni Lampo moved with his wife and family to the Brazos Valley. Again his brothers-in-law had moved ahead of him and had urged him to follow. He farmed wherever he could rent a piece of land until 1902, two years after Sam's birth, when he bought a 107-acre farm at Dilly Shaw. Giovanni Lampo and other Italian immigrants had lived up to their reputations as hard-working and trustworthy. The virtues paid off when Giovanni went to buy his own farm. He had saved $200, which was $800 short of the seller's price. But a businessman and cotton ginner named Sam Parker, Sr. loaned him the whole $1,000 sum — interest free and with no signature — and urged him to keep the $200 savings to feed the Lampo family. Giovanni paid off the debt in two years.

Italians got along better with the Mexicans of the

[12] Johnny and Bonny Lampo, private interview held at 401 Dodge Street, Bryan, Texas, June 22, 1980.

[13] Sam Lampo, *Ibid.*

area than the English-speaking people had. They were both Latin peoples who practiced Catholicism, and it was relatively easy for Italians to learn Spanish since the two languages are somewhat similar. There were also cultural similarities. To all Mediterranean people, food is the symbol of life's chief medium for human beings, the family.[14] Both groups revered the family and practiced patriarchy. The Mexican concept of "virilidad" (manliness) was well understood by Italian males, who knew the term as "virilità." In addition, Mexicans and Italians occupied a subordinate position of prestige, privilege, and power. Most of the Italian, Mexican, and black farm laborers worked together with a minimum of discord. Members of the three groups gathered every year to celebrate "Juneteenth" — the June 19 anniversary date of the black emancipation in Texas. These minorities created a framework of tolerance in their associations: neutrality was the keynote. The people of Sicily had learned to cope with *stranieri* (strangers) in their midst through centuries of foreign domination, which had brought them into contact with Arabs, Normans, Spaniards, Austrians, and many other peoples.

The Sicilians' attitude of tolerance or acceptance of persons unlike themselves may also be explained by a general lack of interest about the world outside their town. *Campanilismo* characterized the southern Italians' identification with their village existence. In Italy, *campanilismo* appears to have been a defense mechanism. While it symbolized attachment to the past, it also reflected a resentment at not being included in the wave of the future — of which the city was the prime manifestation. The villager was envious of the city life and the prestige that accrued to those who had a knowledge of city ways. At the same time he was ever aware of his inability to partake in such a life given the resources at his disposal. The Sicilian farmer in Texas placed himself, his

[14] Herbert J. Gans, *The Urban Villagers.* (New York: The Free Press, 1962), p. 33.

family, and the people from his *paese* (village) as the prime interests within his frame of reference. All else for him was secondary. The indifference with which southern Italians regarded the Mexican, black, and Anglo-American farmers with whom they came in contact, reflected this scale of immediate priorities and led to a minimum of interaction. Nevertheless, it came to pass that many Mexicans worked on Italian farms as sharecroppers, as more and more Italians began to buy their own lands.

In spite of their cooperative work together, social relations between Mexicans and Italians were kept at a distance because of the ethnocentrism of both groups. Each felt that its particular culture was somehow superior to the other, and intermarriage was virtually nonexistent. For the Italians, marriage by endogamous prescription took place only among clan members. But there was not complete harmony among the Italians. Sicilians from the town of Corleone settled on the east side of the Brazos River, and those from Poggioreale made their homes on the west side of the river. The two townspeoples were mutually suspicious of one another in Sicily, and this mistrust continued for some time in America. They spoke different dialects, and worshipped different patron saints. The Poggiorealese prayed to St. Anthony, and the Corleonese prayed to St. Luke. For fifty years, marriage between members of the two clans was very rare.

The Italians bought flood-prone land in the Brazos bottoms between Hearne and Bryan. Earlier settlers, including Germans and Czechs, had avoided it for this reason. The Italians were willing to gamble with disaster in exchange for fertile soil that would normally produce abundant crops. They lost badly in 1899, and again in 1900, when devastating floods struck the region. From June 27 to July 1, 1899, a great rainstorm centered over the Brazos River watershed. It caused the worst flood on record for that area. Between thirty and thirty-five lives were lost, and property damage was estimated at nine million dollars. Robert Falzone, a lifetime resident of the Brazos Valley area, and grandson of Giorgio Falzone, one of the original Italian settlers, described the impact of the 1899 flood on his family: "All of the crops were destroyed. Potatoes and onions were especially vulnerable. My family saved themselves by climbing to the roof of their home until help came." [15]

By the 1890s, Brazos County had one of the largest concentrations of Italian farmers in the United States. There were 553 foreign-born Italians living there in 1900. About that time, a benevolent society known as the *Societa di Colonizzazione Italiana del Texas,* bought over 25,000 acres of land which it divided into fifty-acre lots at Perla and Keechie. The society spent almost a million dollars for the purchase of land and for the acquisition of farm machinery and building materials. The oldest mutual aid society in Brazos County with a charter on file with the Office of the Secretary of State is the *Societa Italiana MB Cristofero Colombo.* This organization was incorporated on August 19, 1905, by ten directors, including M. Scardino, Stefena Aiello, and Giralomo Palazzotto. Article 2 of the charter states, "This association is formed for the purpose of mutual benefit and aiding its members in times of sickness and trouble, engaging in works of benevolence and charity, . . ." [16]

In rural areas such as the Brazos Valley, the patriarchal family unit remained an accepted way of life. Fewer conflicts with tradition existed in these communities than in the urban areas such as Dallas, and Houston, where the roles of men and women became somewhat modified. The immigrant woman was especially slow to change. Because rural Italians lived in colonies, women

[15] Robert Falzone, deputy sheriff, Falls County, private interview held at the County Sheriff's Department, Marlin, Texas, June 21, 1980.

[16] Texas, Office of the Secretary of State, charter of the *Societa Italiana MB Cristofero Colombo.* Charter No. 14683, Austin, Texas, August 9, 1905.

had fewer opportunities to associate with people other than those of their own nationalistic background. Unlike Italians living in large cities in other parts of the country, there were no factories where Italian women could work and achieve a degree of independence from their husbands. Even domestic service was not available in rural Texas, because only a small number of people could afford maids or household servants.

When the Italian ambassador visited Texas in 1905, he was told that Bryan had 3,000 of his countrymen. The entire population of the town at that time was only 5,000.[17] According to Eliot Lord, in the "notable Italian colony at Bryan, Texas, a settlement of Sicilians, numbering about twenty-four hundred, has been prospering for several years. The families are spread over the neighborhood to a distance of eighteen miles from the town, and are, for the most part, proprietors of lands chiefly sown with Indian corn and cotton. The families that rent lands generally pay $5.00 a year per acre, and . . . the families of the owners and tenants save from $100 to $1,000 yearly, according as they are more or less numerous and economical, and as the crops are more or less abundant. The greater part of these families came originally from Trapani in the neighborhood of Palermo, and in point of industry, thrift, good conduct, and prosperity, they need not shun comparison with the immigrants from any other part of Italy or from any other country."[18]

According to Lord, "All the chief food supplies are here abundant and cheap. Meat selling at five cents a pound. Taxation was said to be exceedingly light. The climate was judged to be fully as good as that of Sicily. There is much fertile land to be obtained for cultivation, and the owners give the use of the land without charge for two years to the farmer who clears it. The settlers cut down the trees, selling the wood at $2.00 per cord, and

[17] Rolle, *The Immigrant Upraised, op. cit.*, p. 227.
[18] Eliot Lord, *The Italian in America.* (New York: B. F. Buck, 1905), p. 89.

harvest Indian corn in the first year and cotton in the second." [19]

Antonio Varisco is representative of those robust Italian settlers. He was the son of Biagio Varisco, and Maria Zumma, of Poggioreale. Antonio was born in New Orleans on June 10, 1878. When he was one year old, the family moved back to Italy, but Antonio returned to the United States in 1906. He had married Dorotea Tritico four years earlier, and the couple gave birth to a son, Brazos, on October 12, 1902. Soon after his arrival in America, Antonio found employment in a macaroni factory in Houston. After two months he moved to Bryan and worked for eight months at seventy-five cents a day. Later he rented twenty-five acres of land, and gradually became the owner of more than 1,000 acres of cotton land.

Brazos joined his parents in Bryan in 1907. He married Lucille Scardino in 1924 and became an American citizen five years later. Brazos eventually acquired 3,100 acres of land of which 2,300 acres were devoted to cotton raising. Together with his father, and a brother named Giuseppe, he owned a cotton gin with the capacity for producing 2,000 bales of cotton a year. He also owned five airplanes for agricultural spraying. Brazos served as director of the Bryan Chamber of Commerce, and as a member of the Young Men's Club. He was active in civic affairs and charitable movements.[20] Varisco, Texas, a rural community in west Brazos County, and Varisco airport, which is located in that community are named in his honor.

Sam Emola was a farmer in Corleone, Sicily, before he brought his family to the United States in 1891. High taxes and cost of living had made it necessary for him to look for better conditions, as had most of the European immigrants arriving in America since the 1850s. The

[19] *Ibid.*, p. 90.

[20] Giovanni Schiavo, *Italian-American Who's Who.* Vol. VII (New York: Vigo, 1943), pp. TEX. 4, 5.

ANTONIO and DOROTEA VARISCO with children.
— *Courtesy Brazos Varisco. From a copy at U.T.*
The Institute of Texan Cultures

Emolas followed many Sicilians sailing from Palermo to New Orleans, then moving toward the Texas Gulf Coast area or the Brazos Valley. In Brazos County he farmed "on the halves" until he saved enough money to purchase his own land.[21]

In 1896 a parish was established for the large number of Italian families who had moved to Bryan. St. Anthony Catholic Church was erected on Polk Avenue, the white frame building serving until 1926 when it was destroyed by fire. Most of the Italians who settled in the Brazos Valley brought with them a religious custom, the Feast of St. Joseph, celebrated on March 19. St. Joseph is the patron saint of Italy, and particularly of Sicily. Dishes for the feast had to be prepared of fish, pasta, eggs, and vegetables. Since the dinner was held during Lent, no meat was allowed. Fancy cakes and biscuits were elaborately decorated by the women of the church who worked for days preparing for the celebration. On the day before the feast the priest was called to bless the food and drink.

On the feast day families would invite the poor to come into their homes to eat. The master of the house would symbolically bathe the feet of the guests as done before the Last Supper. After the feast the remaining food was distributed to the poor. When the Sicilians reached Texas, the custom was altered somewhat when the people could speak no English and felt awkward about inviting people who could not understand the language or custom. They chose, instead, children of their own families to represent the poor.[22]

No study of the Italian emigrants from the *Mezzogiorno*. who settled in Texas would be complete without examining the importance of the roles played by Italian women. The Italian woman has been the center of the life of the entire ethnic group. The privileges transmitted to

[21] Mary E. Dorsey, *Those Were The Days: Bryan-Brazos County-1821-1921*. (Bryan: Fuller, 1976), p. 43.

[22] *Ibid.*, pp. 24-25.

her gave her a status which evoked the special position of women in the legend of chivalry. At the same time the responsibilities, demands, and expectations placed upon her were enormous. The stresses on her that resulted were staggering. As Professor Richard Gambino, of Queens College, has aptly put it: "While all Italian-Americans feel the poignancy of their inherited sensitivity to the essential hardness of life, the woman experiences it deeply, almost physically, in ways which the male is spared." [23]

The experience of Angela Salvaggio Cangelosi provides an excellent example. Angela Salvaggio was born on September 5, 1855, in Poggioreale, Province of Trapani. She married Giovanni Cangelosi, and the couple in time had three sons and two daughters. In the 1880s the family moved to the Brazos County area where Giovanni's brother Giuseppe already lived. The Cangelosis settled in the area known as Mudville between Mumford, Steele Store, and Stone City, near Bryan. Giovanni purchased about 260 acres of Brazos River bottom land. With the building of a wooden house, Angela's life became that of a typical pioneer woman of the day: preparing meals, sewing, washing, cleaning, educating her children, and rearing them in the knowledge of the Savior.

Frank E. Tritico, great-grandson of Angela Salvaggio Cangelosi, describes her toilsome life in the book *Women in Early Texas.* "Up at dawn, Angela prepared the day's meals and sent breakfast and lunch to the men and boys in the fields by their younger sisters and brothers. The staple Italian meal of *pasta* (spaghetti) had to be rolled by hand and placed in the sun to dry . . . Bread was made by hand and baked in outdoor ovens of brick heated by coals. The first year the cooking was done in the fireplace which served as the house's heating unit also. Special grills and cooking pots which sat in coals and had coals heaped above served as cooking utensils . . . Large

[23] Richard Gambino, *Blood Of My Blood.* (New York: Anchor, 1975), p. 160.

iron wash pots were placed over fires outdoors. The family's clothes, washed by hand, went into the pot where they were stirred with a stick, rinsed, and hung in the sun to dry. The soap used had been made by Angela from lye and grease renderings. Later the clothes were ironed by Angela and the girls with flat irons heated in the fireplace or stove." [24]

Dr. Tritico points out the many important functions performed by Angela, and other dedicated Italian women. Most of the clothes were made at home: dresses, boys' and men's shirts, and even everyday trousers. Lace was crocheted and tatted by the women in the evenings by firelight or lamplight to be used as trimmings on the girls' and ladies' dresses. "Angela and John were very religious and since there was no church near, they gathered the family and the relatives on Sunday mornings and read the Mass and Gospel from a missal brought from Sicily. Evening devotions were led by Angela after supper in front of the fireplace . . . The hardships of pioneering were alleviated in part by the regular Sunday evening dances Angela arranged in her home where one of her sons played the accordion and friends and neighbors brought their adolescents to dance and visit. There were no doctors in the area and Angela was much sought after as a midwife and *doctoressa (sic)*. She made home-remedies and used folk-medicine and herbs in treating her family and those who came to her for help." [25] Angela died in Houston in 1924.

The next generation of Italian women living in Texas had easier lives. A few of them even earned fame and fortune. For example, the success achieved by Josephina Lucchese is quite remarkable. Her father, Salvatore Lucchese was born into a boot-making family near Palermo, Sicily, in 1866. In 1882, he landed at Galveston and settled a year later in San Antonio, opening a boot shop. He

[24] Evelyn M. Carrington (et al.) *Women in Early Texas.* (Austin: Jenkins, 1975), p. 45.

[25] *Ibid.,* pp. 46-47.

married, and Josephina was born in San Antonio in 1893. Josephina began her career as a coloratura soprano with a New York debut in 1922, and was an instant success. In 1930-31, she toured North America for six months, then traveled to Europe where she gave 150 operatic and concert performances in Holland, Germany, Italy, Denmark, Czechoslovakia, and Switzerland. She returned to America and became the leading coloratura soprano of the Philadelphia Grand Opera Company. She was on the music faculty at the University of Texas from 1957 until 1970, when she retired.

After the turn of the century, immigrant settlements spread to the vicinity of Highbank in Falls County, and into Burleson and Robertson counties. This outward thrust of settlement along the Brazos River appears to have been the result of the rising population of the Brazos County community, which caused the price of good farmland to increase. Thus, some Italians moved toward more recently settled areas where the land was cheaper.[26] For the most part, the farmland of these people has been retained in family hands. When farming cotton and other crops became unprofitable for small family farmers, the children moved into the towns of Bryan, Hearne, and Marlin and engaged in other kinds of businesses. Meanwhile, Italians were also settling on the Galveston County mainland.

THE ITALIANS OF THE
GALVESTON COUNTY MAINLAND

Italians from southern Italy began settling on the Galveston County mainland in the late 1890s. While searching the parish records of the Shrine of the True Cross Catholic Church, at Dickinson, Texas, for the old-

[26] Brazos, Falls, Burleson, and Robertson Counties, "Reverse Index to Deeds," "General Index to Deeds." Several volumes were consulted in each county, in order to determine changes in land ownership between 1881-1926.

DICKINSON, TEXAS

Photo by Schlueter, Courtesy Beulah Owens Hughes,
Copy From U.T. Institute of Texan Cultures,
San Antonio, Texas

est document involving an Italian, the author discovered a Certificate of Baptism for Joseph Pizzitolla, who was baptized on April 4, 1897. He was the son of Gustavo Pizzitolla, and Anna Ciulla, of Texas City.[27] Many Italians were brought to the Galveston County mainland by the Stewart Title Company. Others went there from Bryan to seek relief from the June 27-July 1, 1899, rainstorm. At the time they were not aware that from September 8-9, 1900, a great hurricane would strike Galveston and kill between 6,000 and 8,000 persons. They had figuratively moved *de fumo in flammam* (out of the smoke into the flame). The Italian consular agent, Clemente Nicolini, aided the flood victims in finding new lands in Dickinson, and elsewhere in Galveston County. For a while, he operated what amounted to a one-man immigration bureau and land development company. Nicolini Street in Dickinson is named in his honor.[28]

In 1905, the Italian government sent its ambassador in Washington, Baron Mayor des Planches, to visit Dickinson and Galveston, as part of his trip through the southern United States. His major purpose was to discover suitable resettlement areas for Italians living in the northern part of the United States, who desired to take advantage of the agricultural opportunities of the South and Southwest.[29] About 200 Brazos Valley Italians moved to the Dickinson area. They bought some fairly inexpensive land, and began raising fruit commercially. During the first and second decades of this century, Italians in Dickinson shipped tens of thousands of cases of strawberries in refrigerated boxcars to markets throughout the Midwest. They also began raising figs commercially in the 1920s.

[27] Texas, certificate of baptism issued April 4, 1897, recorded in the Shrine of the True Cross Catholic Church, Dickinson, Texas.

[28] Institute of Texan Cultures, *The Italian Texans, op. cit.,* pp. 22-23.

[29] Jim Hudson, *Dickinson: Taller Than The Pines.* (Burnet, Texas: Nortex, 1979), pp. 87-88.

ITALIAN SCHOOL BOYS in Dickinson, Texas ca. 1913
— Courtesy Beulah Owens Hughes, Dickinson, Texas
Copy From U.T. Institute of Texan Cultures,
San Antonio, Texas

The families of Francesco Termini, Andrea Magliolo, and Leo Luca Liggio offer examples of the many Italians who have prospered and made important contributions to Galveston County. Francesco Termini was born in Italy on October 28, 1873. He was thirteen years old when he arrived in America. Later he operated a small grocery store, his business expanded, and he bought and developed a considerable amount of land in Dickinson and Galveston. Eventually, he played an important role in helping to develop the business community of Dickinson. Termini Street in Dickinson is named in his honor. Andrea Magliolo arrived in Galveston in 1905 from the island of Favignana, which is located off the west coast of Sicily. At the time he was seventeen, and spoke no English. Andrea worked as a barber in the shop of his future brother-in-law, Rosario Vassallo, and in 1911 he borrowed enough money to open up his own business. Two years earlier, he had married Grazia Vassallo, and the couple had five sons and two daughters. Four of the sons became physicians and opened clinics in Dickinson and League City.[30]

Leo Luca Liggio was born in Corleone, Sicily. He married a lady with the forename of Benedetta in 1875, and the couple had three daughters and two sons. Leo and his eldest son Vincenzo sailed to New York in 1891. Then they traveled by train to a small town in Louisiana, and worked in a sawmill there for two years. The other members of their family joined them in Louisiana. The Liggios moved to Bryan and labored as sharecroppers until 1899 when they, and other Italian families, migrated to Dickinson. The men worked for the G.H.&H. Railroad on trackage which eventually connected Galveston and Houston. In 1906, Leo and his friend, Giuseppe Scalisi, purchased ten acres of land on which they grew strawberries and other crops. Leo became a naturalized citizen of the United States in 1913, and

[30] *Ibid.,* pp. 103-104.

opened the first movie house in Dickinson two years later. His son Vincenzo, who was born in 1876, married Paulene Reele on June 25, 1905. Vincenzo became a respected businessman in Dickinson, and Liggio Street is named after him.[31]

In 1909, Professor Alberto Pecorini, of the American International College, at Springfield, Massachusetts, reported that "... nearly one thousand Italians reside in the vicinity of Dickinson. They are raising vegetables and berries, and the majority are quite well off; the colony increases very rapidly." [32] Three years later Ambassador Mayor des Planches made another visit to Texas. He indicated that the Italian colony at Dickinson "... includes about 100 families, all from the province of Palermo. Each one possesses from four to ten acres of excellent land, well cultivated, worth $100 to $200 per acre." [33] The ambassador found similar settlements at Hitchcock and Galveston. "Galveston has at present about 30,000 inhabitants of which perhaps 1,200 are Italians." [34] While Italians from southern Italy were struggling to make a living in the Brazos Valley, and on the Galveston County mainland, men and women from northern Italy were establishing farms in Montague County.

THE ITALIAN SETTLEMENT
IN MONTAGUE COUNTY

The 937-square-mile area of Montague County was known to French trappers and traders and to Spanish government officials because of the important Taovaya

---

[31] Josephina Marie Liggio, private interview held at 4124 Liggio Street, Dickinson, Texas, July 6, 1980; Letter from Josephina Marie Liggio, Dickinson, August 3, 1980.

[32] Alberto Pecorini, "The Italian as an Agricultural Laborer," *The Annals of The American Academy of Political and Social Science.* Vol. XXXIII, January-June, 1909, p. 388.

[33] Edmondo Mayor des Planches, *Attraverso gli Stati Uniti Per l'emigrazione italiana.* (Torino: Unione tipografico-editrice torinese, 1913), pp. 164-168.

[34] *Ibid.,* p. 165.

**L. to R.: John Ulbig, Anthony Paul (Tony the Rep.) Fenoglio, and
Frank Ulbig. Oil Rig in Montague, Texas.**

— Courtesy Fill Fenoglio, Montague, Texas
Copy From U.T. Institute of Texan Cultures,
San Antonio, Texas

rancheria located in a bend of the Red River in the northern part of the present county. Later known as Spanish Fort, the rancheria was probably visited by French traders as early as 1719. In October, 1759, Diego Ortiz Parrilla led a Spanish punitive expedition across the county to the fortified rancheria and was defeated there by allied Indians flying a French flag. After 1812, the Indian settlements diminished in size and importance. The Chihuahua Trail of 1839, the old California Trail, and the Butterfield Overland Mail Route all passed through Montague County. Old Red River Station, possibly the first settlement in the area, was an early crossing place, and in the 1870s the station was used by attendants of the herds of Longhorn cattle, as they followed the Chisholm Trail to northern markets.

The earliest Anglo-American settlers known to have located in Montague County were Henry Bradern and John Keenan in 1854. Then at the first county election in August, 1858, a site to be called Montague and to be located at the geographical center of the county won the election as the county seat. The population of Montague County was 885 in 1870.[35] Italians from the Alpine provinces of northern Italy began arriving in Montague County in the late 1870s. While searching the parish records of St. Mary's Catholic Church at Henrietta, Texas, the author discovered a Certificate of Baptism for Rose Fenoglio, who was born on July 26, 1879. This is the oldest church record involving an Italian in Montague County. She was the daughter of Jacob and Domenica Fenoglio, and the child was baptized in Montague on September 28, 1893.[36] The Fenoglios came from the village of Spraco Sano, which is located in Turin Province, in the region of Piedmont. Their forefathers had worked in the coal mines of Valle d'Aosta. Giovanni and Antonio

[35] Fannie C. Potter (Bellows), *History of Montague County.* (Austin: E. L. Steck, 1913), pp. 133-146.

[36] Texas, certificate of baptism issued September 28, 1893, recorded in St. Mary's Catholic Church, Henrietta, Texas.

Fenoglio left Italy for the opportunity of making more money and improving their standards of living. They sailed to New York from Le Havre, France, and went to Braidwood, Illinois, to find employment mining coal. From there they moved to Lehigh, Oklahoma, and again worked in the coal mines.

THE OKLAHOMA INTERLUDE

The coal deposits of Oklahoma that attracted Italian immigrants were not developed until the 1870s. The first Italians entered the region in 1875, and two or three hundred were in the vicinity in 1883. Pittsburg County had the largest number of all immigrants in the coal-producing area and the second highest in the state with 3,367 listed in 1910. Of these foreign-born residents the Italians were by far the largest single nationality, numbering 1,398. The principal Italian colony in the county, as well as the state, was in Krebs. Coal County ranked second in the number of Italian settlers. Lehigh, where the Fenoglio group worked, was established in 1880, as the first coal camp in the county. Mine owners moved the site several times, eventually locating the permanent town in 1884. Two years later, Coalgate was founded. Although not as dominant as in Krebs, the foreign stock numbered 1,206 out of 3,255. Other nearby towns, such as Phillips and Midway, soon developed. As in Pittsburg County, Italians were the largest group, numbering 443. Along with the second generation and several undesignated Italians from the old Austrian Tyrol, approximately 700 lived in the county.

Living conditions in the coal-mining communities of Oklahoma left much to be desired, particularly during the days of Indian Territory. When the first Italians drifted to the area, few houses were available in this generally unsettled country of the Choctaw Indians. As a result, the miners almost totally depended on the "company" to meet their material needs. They lived in company houses,

ANTONIO FENOGLIO
— Courtesy Fill Fenoglio, Montague, Texas
Copy From U.T. Institute of Texan Cultures,
San Antonio, Texas

and were sometimes paid in scrip good only in the company store. The houses were usually one-story, one-family dwellings, containing from three to five rooms. Poorly built with cheap lumber, these homes were little more than shacks.[37]

SOUTH TO TEXAS

Giovanni and Antonio Fenoglio became dissatisfied with the living and working conditions of Lehigh. Like the Sicilian settlers of the Brazos Valley, these fair-skinned, blue-eyed Alpine Italians developed a strong desire to acquire and farm their own land. In 1876, three families headed by the two Fenoglio brothers, and Barretto Raimondi, moved from Oklahoma to Pilot Grove, a small community in Grayson County, Texas.[38] The small group settled on 640 acres of land which they thought they had purchased. But after paying most of the $3,000 agreed upon for a section of the land, it became apparent that the three men had been swindled, and did not have title to the property they had cleared and worked. Strangers in a strange land, unable to speak English well, and not having access to legal counsel, they gave up their claim and headed west towards Wichita Falls.

The three families stopped to rest near Montague, and developed a liking for the area with its sandy soil that was perfect for vineyards, orchards, and vegetable farms. Thus, Montague County became their home. In spite of the problem of maintaining an adequate supply of water to meet the needs of their families and crops, the group prospered in farming. They wrote to their kinfolk and friends about the outstanding agricultural opportunities of the area. These people were impressed, and some of them migrated to Montague, Bowie, and Nocona. Pete Belisario moved from Osage City, Kansas, to

[37] Kenny L. Brown, *The Italians in Oklahoma.* (Norman: University of Oklahoma Press, 1980), pp. 12, 14, 42.

[38] Melvin Fenoglio, private interview held at Box 13, Montague, Texas, June 29, 1980.

Montague in 1890; and Tony Rossi also went there that year. Then Giovanni Carminati, Paul Veretto, and Pete Carminati and their families arrived shortly thereafter. Around 1900, other Italians settled in the area. Among them were the families of John Vitali, Decio Gasparini, Andrew Pelligrenelli, Edward Aragoni, Bartolo Salvi, and Battista Salvi.[39]

Giovanni and Delfina Carminati were typical of these people. Giovanni was born in Bergamo, near Milan, in the region of Lombardy about 1875. While in Italy he had worked as a day laborer for between fifteen and thirty cents a day. Giovanni arrived in Kansas *via* New York about 1887, and worked in the coal mines of Pittsburg. He moved to Montague in the early 1890s, where he met and married Marietta Tonetti. The couple had eight children. In Montague, the family cut down trees and sold the wood, and then bought a small farm. For a time, Giovanni served as a trustee of the local school.[40] When Marietta died, Giovanni went back to Italy and married Delfina Tonetti on February 15, 1925. He brought Delfina to Montague on May 20, 1925, and the couple eventually had two children.

Delfina Tonetti Carminati was born on December 11, 1896, in Brusnengo, near Vercelli, in the region of Piedmont. Her life was that of a typical pioneer woman of the day: preparing meals, sewing, washing, cleaning, educating her children, and rearing them in the knowledge of the Savior. Up at dawn, Delfina prepared the day's meals and sent breakfast and lunch to the men and boys in the fields by their younger sisters and brothers. A typical evening meal prepared by Delfina might begin with *minestrone alla milanese* (vegetable soup, Milanese style), followed by *stracotto* (pot roast), served with *po-*

[39] Melvin Fenoglio, "Strangers In A Strange Land," in Alva B. Copeland (et al.), *Panorama of Nocona's Trade area.* (St. Jo, Texas: S.J.T. Printing Company, 1976), p. 122.

[40] Joe Louis Carminati, private interview held at Box 157, Montague, Texas, July 16, 1980.

BARNEY FENOGLIO homestead near Montague, Texas.

— *Courtesy of Mrs. C. P. Nabours, Montague, Texas*
From U. T. Institute of Texas Cultures,
San Antonio, Texas

lenta e osei (a cornmeal dish with a sauce of tiny wild birds), and *risotto* (a rice dish cooked in broth). The food ordinarily was accompanied by delightful homemade tangy wine made from concord grapes. A favorite dessert was *zabaglione* (a sweet made with beaten eggs and Marsala wine). Most of the clothes were made at home: dresses, boys' shirts, and even everyday trousers. Lace was crocheted and tatted by the women in the evenings by firelight or lamplight to be used as trimmings on the girls' and ladies' dresses.[41]

The lives of the Italian population of Montague County revolved around agriculture. They originally purchased land at six dollars to eight dollars an acre, with mineral rights included. Oil discoveries on several tracts have since enhanced property values considerably.[42] Some of the original settlers became grocers, butchers, carpenters, etc. Most of these immigrants were devout Catholics, and in 1901 they established St. John's Catholic Church in Montague. Previous to the erection of the church, regular services were held in various homes. A priest occasionally visited the community and offered mass, and this was an opportunity for baptisms, marriages, and other church rituals. Sometimes, a temporary altar was set up outdoors to accommodate large gatherings for Sunday worship.

Table IX shows the number of foreign-born Italians resident in Montague County between 1880 and 1940. The Table indicates an increase every decade between 1880 and 1920, and a decline between 1920 and 1940. The Italian colony reached a peak of sixty-six foreign-born in 1920, and the total population of Italian immigrants and their families was estimated at 300 in the first quarter of the twentieth century. Figure I is a time series relationship which gives the number of foreign-born Italians re-

[41] Delfina Carminati, private interview held at Montague, Texas, July 16, 1980.

[42] Institute of Texan Cultures, *The Italian Texans, op. cit.,* pp. 15-16.

WEDDING OF T. J. Lampson and Mary Cangelosi. Stafford, Texas. 1927

— *Courtesy Frank E. Tritico*
Copy From U.T. Institute of Texan Cultures,

siding in Montague County between 1880 and 1940. The graph indicates that the sharpest climb in the Italian population occurred between 1890 and 1900, and the greatest decline occurred between 1920 and 1930. Most of these people were hard-working, law-abiding citizens. But they sometimes experienced prejudices from their Protestant neighbors, who were suspicious of their customs and religious practices. According to Melvin Fenoglio, a lifetime resident of Montague, "Despite their encounters with hardships in establishing a new home in an alien environment, the majority of the early new citizens possessed a happy temperament. Courageous in facing their many problems, forthright in their responsibilities as citizens, and optimistic in their outlooks toward the future, they began to bridge the gap which separated them and their American neighbors." [43]

TABLE IX. Foreign-born Italians Resident
in Montague County: 1880-1940.

Year	No. of Italians
1880	none listed
1890	12
1900	39
1910	52
1920	66
1930	39
1940	25

Sources: United States Census Office, Tenth Census of the United States (1880), Population, Volume I, Washington, D.C., 1883, p. 530.

Eleventh Census of the United States (1890), Population, Volume I, Part I, Washington, D.C., 1895, p. 662.

Twelfth Census of the United States (1900), Population, Part I, Washington, D.C., 1901, p. 785.

Thirteenth Census of the United States (1910), Population, Volume III, Washington, D.C., 1913, p. 836.

[43] Fenoglio, "Strangers In A Strange Land," *op. cit.,* p. 123.

Fourteenth Census of the United States (1920), Population, Volume III, Washington, D.C., 1922, p. 1023.

Fifteenth Census of the United States (1930), Population, Volume III, Part II, Washington, D.C., 1932, p. 1018.

Sixteenth Census of the United States (1940), Population, Volume II, Part VI, Washington, D.C., 1943, p. 900.

At first, the Italians tended to associate exclusively with members of their own group. Marriage, by endogamous prescription, took place only among clan members. But this practice was gradually abandoned by later generations. Weekly dances were a favorite form of diversion. Four couples and sometimes twelve or sixteen couples danced to *il codiglione*.[44] In the beginning, dances were closed to outsiders, as Italian dances were replaced by contemporary American dances. Men played *bocce* and *morra*[45] regularly on Sunday afternoons, especially in the summertime. It was customary for families to take turns preparing huge feasts which included many kinds of food and wine. All clan members were invited, and after dinner the games began.

Figure I. Foreign-Born Italians Resident in Montague County: 1880-1940.

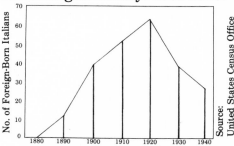

[44] *il codiglione* — a folk dance common in some parts of *Alta Italia*.

[45] *bocce* — a game somewhat resembling bowls. *morra* — a game played by two people in which both simultaneously extend some of the fingers of one hand, and immediately pick a number from zero to ten. The person who guesses the total number of extended fingers is the winner.

Figure II. Representatives of Italian Families Buried at St. William's Catholic Cemetery, Montague, Texas

Immigrants	Dates of birth and death	Important Epitaphs
James Arami	Nov. 8, 1896- Mar. 19, 1954	
Antonio Betazza	Aug. 19, 1871- Jan. 2, 1953	
John Carminati	Apr. 29, 1875- Oct. 13, 1954	
John B. Corado	Sept. 6, 1849- May 28, 1917	
Jack Fenoglio	Apr. 1, 1844- Mar. 28, 1922	"Founder of Montague Italian Colony."
Pete Giaketti	Oct. 12. 1881- Jan. 25, 1965	
Dasio Gasparino	Jan. 15, 1867- Mar. 7, 1946	
Louis Guiliani	Jan. 28, 1882- Dec. 4, 1920	
August Nobili	Feb. 10, 1883- July 22, 1976	
Mollie Pellissero	July 26, 1873- July 26, 1914	
Barrett(o) Raymond(i)	Oct. 8, 1841- Mar. 5, 1915	
Rocco Reibaldi	Nov. 1852- Dec. 25, 1903	
Santina Rossi	Mar. 20, 1851- Sept. 10, 1922	
Antonio Rotta	Mar. 20, 1871- Mar. 21, 1937	
Batista Salvi	Apr. 3, 1882- July 8, 1965	
Paul Veretto	Jan. 17, 1855- Mar. 25, 1916	
Florence Vicari	July 29, 1870- Jan. 9, 1934	
Nellie Vitali	Feb. 15, 1879- June 14, 1915	

Source: Investigation conducted by the author on July 20, 1981. One representative of every Italian family buried in the cemetery is included. The family member with the oldest birth date was selected. Some one hundred tombstones in the graveyard contain Italian surnames. This represents about ninety percent of all of the tombstones in the cemetery.

Although the Italians of Montague County initially felt more secure with their native language and customs, they gradually began to adapt to their new environment. Realizing that Texas was now their home, they slowly assimilated the local culture and mores. Italians enrolled their children in public schools, encouraged them to learn the English language, and instilled in them a feeling of patriotism for America. For the most part, the farmland of these settlers has been retained in family hands. But the Italians of Montague County also have become leaders in business, industry, and the professions. Tony Fenoglio served in the Texas State Legislature from 1951 to 1961, and Melvin Fenoglio was superintendent of the Montague Independent School District in the 1970s and early 1980s.

The county clerk's office of Montague County is a treasure trove containing countless gems of information about the Italians who settled in that area. The author examined many documents and unearthed some information. But future work by a resident scholar is needed to extract, compile, and analyze the hundreds of other documents located there. The oldest birth certificate for an Italian was for Antonio H. Fenoglio, who was born on April 24, 1881. He was the son of Barney Fenoglio and Teresa Enrietta Fenoglio.[46] The oldest deed recorded for a person of Italian lineage was for the purchase of 200 acres of land in Montague County by Decimus et Ultimus Barziza of Harris County. Barziza purchased the land from W. C. Wilson, also of Harris County for a sum of three hundred dollars. The date of the instrument was January 19, 1871, and it was filed on September 26, 1874.[47]

[46] Texas, certificate of baptism, issued April 24, 1881. Certificate number 1535. Office of the county clerk, Montague County.

[47] Texas, Montague County, Deed Record Volume C., pp. 118-119; Reverse Index to Deeds, A-K 1-2-3, p. 22.

Barziza was the son of Viscount Filippo Ignacio, a Venetian who had settled at Williamsburg, Virginia, in 1814. His son, Decimus et Ultimus, became a lawyer and banker in Texas,[48] but there is no evidence to indicate that he ever resided in Montague County. The oldest deed recorded for a native Italian who made Montague County his home was for the purchase of three acres of land by Antonio Fenoglio, who bought the property from N. C. Smith on September 19, 1887.[49] Between 1892 and 1897, Fenoglio purchased more than 106 acres of additional lands.

MINOR ITALIAN COLONIES

At the beginning of World War I, there were approximately 15,000 Italians in Texas, and about two-thirds of them were farmers. In addition to the major colonies around Bryan, Dickinson, and Montague, there were smaller settlements in the state. One hundred families near Houston were growing vegetables and fruits, and many of these people owned the lands they cultivated. Italian families were also engaged in successful truck farming in the vicinity of Dallas and Austin. Nicola Negro and the Destefno brothers offer examples of early Italian pioneers who settled on the outskirts of Dallas. Nicola Negro arrived in the vicinity of Dallas in 1887, and eventually established a large produce business in the city. He was one of the first persons to recommend the refrigeration of bananas in transit, and he received the first refrigerated shipment of the fruit from New Orleans. Francesco and Achille Destefno came to Texas in 1873. They worked in the wholesale fruit and produce business in Dallas, and made a small fortune at this enterprise.[50]

[48] Decimus et Ultimus Barziza, *The Adventures of a Prisoner of War: 1863-1864*. Edited by R. Henderson, (Shuffler: Austin, 1964), pp. 1-18.

[49] Texas, Montague County, Deed Record Volume 2., p. 558; Reverse Index to Deeds, A-K 1-2-3, p. 166.

[50] University of Texas at San Antonio, Institute of Texan Cul-

JIM FALSONE
— Courtesy Mrs. Riestino, Plantation Dehydrating Co.
Bryan, Texas. Copy From U.T. Institute of
Texan Cultures, San Antonio, Texas

Meanwhile, about one hundred families were working on small farms near the city of San Antonio. Several colonization experiments by Italians in northern Texas failed because of a scarcity of water there. The one notable exception was in Montague County. In southeast Texas some Italians grew rice, and others became vineyardists in the neighborhood of Gunnison.[51] The first licensed winery in Texas is operated by the Qualia (Quaglia) family on Hudson Road in Del Rio. Francesco and Maria Quaglia started the enterprise in 1883. Initially they only made wine for their family as they had done in their native village near Milan, Italy. The winery now produces about 5,000 gallons of the beverage annually, from grapes grown on an eighteen-acre tract of land.[52]

RACISM AND PREJUDICE

As pointed out, Italians got along better with the Mexicans of the area than the English-speaking people had because the two groups shared important cultural similarities. But what about their relationships with black and Anglo-American settlers? Contacts between tures, "Dallas Pioneers," San Antonio, Texas.

[51] Rolle, *The Immigrant Upraised, op. cit.,* p. 226; Pecorini, "The Italian as an Agricultural Laborer," *op. cit.,* p. 388.

[52] Institute of Texan Cultures, *The Italian Texans, op. cit.,* p. 17.

the new immigrants and Anglo-Americans were initially limited to economic transactions. The immigrant furnished his labor in exchange for wages, with which he hoped to start a small farm or business in America or Italy. For many years, the two groups did not take part in mutual social activities.

At first, Italian laborers were employed at wages generally less than those paid to black workers, the people at the lowest level of the economy. They were, in effect, beasts of burden, utilized to generate profits in the fields, mines, and railroads where they toiled. Texas needed cheap labor, and Italians were willing to fill this need. Peasant farmers from a country in which property was scarce would do almost anything to acquire a plot of land.

The Sicilians remained in areas that were prone to flooding for a variety of cultural, social, and economic reasons. They could afford only the cheapest, and therefore worst, farmland. In addition, it was the only fertile land not already under cultivation by earlier arrivals. Most importantly, the Sicilians chose to live close to one another on farms or in labor camps, for the sake of a sense of security. Within the bounds of the Italian community were relatives, close friends, and mutual reinforcement. To Brazos Valley Italians, the possibility of flooding seemed less forboding than the omni-present alien culture which surrounded them. Italians felt helpless outside of their colonies owing to their lack of knowledge of the language, customs, and laws of the new land. Maria Piccolo of El Paso recorded her experiences and feelings in coping with the new environment in a letter to her sister Giovanna, who remained in their native village of Salaparuta. Excerpts from Giovanna's response, written in Italian and dated March 4, 1912, give some indication of Maria's sentiments:

"My Dearest Sister,

I can readily understand the fears and hopes you expressed to me in your last letter. Here in Salaparuta life is very difficult, but our future seems more certain . . . How barren El Paso seems in contrast to the lush fields you have left. . . . I am happy that you, Pietro and the children are eating well and managing to save some money with which to buy a business of your own. It is wonderful that you have acquired so many new things in Texas . . . I pray that your health will soon improve and that your destiny contains much happiness for you . . ."

The early Sicilian settlers in Texas did not discriminate on the basis of racial characteristics. This is because in southern Italy there are people of varying complexions. Thus, Blacks and Italians worked together harmoniously. Overlooking the racial prejudices of the South, Italians sometimes refused to participate in attempts to hold down Blacks. Instead they proposed that both whites and Blacks look with less prejudice at their mutual problems of making a living. Eventually, Italian ignorance of the depth of southern racial feelings helped incite stronger prejudices against them. However, the Italian immigrants, especially those interested in upward social mobility, began to acquire prejudices against Blacks through the acculturation process. As they adopted the values and stereotypes of the dominant, southern Anglo-American group, their comrades in work, *gli neri* (the Blacks) became "niggers" to them. What a shame!

The exploitive work that greeted the immigrants became accompanied by anti-Italian biogtry. Some Anglo-Americans distrusted Roman Catholicism, foreigners and cheap immigrant labor. Bigots emerged to harrass the immigrants with pranks, insults, and vandalism. Occasionally, these incidents led to brawls. Early labor struggles frequently led to outbursts of violence. An episode which occurred during the building of the Midland

Railroad from Paris to Greenville, Texas, provides an example. Italians were employed in the rock quarry to gather rocks to be crushed and spread along the new tracks. In January, 1897, there was an encounter between Italian and American laborers a few miles south of Paris. Some of the Italians were harshly criticized by a teamster named Mr. Clark for the "careless" way in which they were unloading a stone from his wagon. The Italian paid no attention, and he cursed them. One of them started after him with a shovel, and he ran. Six other Italians joined in the chase. They ran Clark into the engine room and seized him and tried to throw him into the drive-rod, which would have crushed him. Mr. Butts, the engineer, and Mr. Nevill, the fireman, came to Clark's aid. Other Italians working at another part of the quarry rushed up with picks and shovels, and more Americans rallied to one another's assistance. During the row one of the Italians was severely stabbed. The sheriff of Lamar County investigated the affair, but no arrests were made.[53]

CONCLUSION

Many Italians were attracted to Texas because of the opportunity to buy and farm their own lands. They contributed much to the agricultural development of the state.

[53] *Greenville Messenger,* January 11, 1897, p. 1.

SELECTED WORKS OF
ITALIAN ARTISTS IN TEXAS

All passes. Art alone
Enduring stays to us; — Henry Austin
Dobson, Ars Victrix, 214:3

The skill and genius of Italian artists and writers, builders, and thinkers — and the judgment and generosity of their patrons — were crucial to the cultural development of Western civilization. Dante, Petrarch, and Boccaccio molded an Italian literary language from their native Tuscan dialect, but their words, translated into many languages, have become part of the common store of the Western literary heritage. The universal genius of Leonardo da Vinci and Michelangelo sets them beyond the limits of category and chronology. They and Giotto, Donatello, Botticelli, and Raphael — to name but a few of the greatest artists of the Renaissance — shaped a new image of man in Western art.

The Italian heritage has touched every aspect of modern American culture. Students of the fine arts at most major Texas universities take courses in the Italian language and literature, as well as Italian art and music. Many Texas art museums contain works by Italian masters. They also house paintings by Texans who have studied art in Italy, such as Mabel H. Brooks, Edward G. Eisenlohr, and Boyer Gonzales. The famous Texas sculptress, Elizabet Ney, worked in Italy and was a close friend of General Giuseppe Garibaldi.[1] Pauline A. Pinck-

---

[1] Esse Forrester-O'Brien, *Art and Artists of Texas.* (Dallas: Tardy, 1935), pp. 58, 94, 109, 266.

ney mentions the influence of Italian painters such Giuseppe Bononi, and Antonio Correggio, on nineteenth-century Texas compositions in her book, *Painting in Texas: The Nineteenth Century.*[2] But Italians had their greatest impact on Texas art in the sculpting of state monuments.

LOUIS AMATEIS (1855-1913)

Standing prominently in the heart of Galveston is one of the greatest monuments in Texas. Erected by Italian-born Louis Amateis, it is known as "Heroes of the Texas Revolution." The monument is seventy-four feet in height and thirty-four feet square at the base. Four monolith columns support a colossal, twenty-two foot bronze figure of Victory. With her right hand extended, Victory holds a laurel wreath and is about to crown the heroes who fought for Texas independence. In her left hand she holds a rose-entwined sword, symbolic of the peace which the hard-earned victory secured. She faces Galveston Bay. Four words are engraved on the entablature: PATRIOTISM, HONOR, DEVOTION, and COURAGE. On the base are medallion portraits of Sam Houston and Stephen F. Austin, and bas-reliefs of "The Surrender of Santa Anna," "The Siege of the Alamo," "The Massacre of Goliad," and the "Battle of San Jacinto." There is also a frieze of medallion portraits of sixteen Texas patriots. Bronze statues representing "Defiance," on the east side, and "Peace," on the west complete this great epic in bronze and granite.[3]

Amateis was born in Turin (Piedmont) in 1855. He became a renowned sculptor in Europe and the Royal Academy of Turin awarded him a gold medal and a silver medal for his extraordinary work. Amateis came to America in 1883 and executed beautiful busts of Andrew

[2] Pauline A. Pinckney, *Painting in Texas: The Nineteenth Century*, (Austin: University of Texas Press, 1967), pp. 71, 98.

[3] Forrester-O'Brien, *Art and Artists of Texas, op. cit.*, pp. 285-286.

Carnegie, President Chester A. Arthur, James G. Blaine, and General Winfield S. Hancock.[4] From 1892 to 1899 he was a professor of Fine Arts at the Columbian University (now George Washington University). He designed a pair of bronze doors for the U.S. Capitol, and constructed three more monuments in Galveston: the "Confederate Monument," the "Rosenberg Statue," and the "Magruder Monument." Amateis died in Washington, D.C., in 1913.

ENRICO CERRACHIO (1880-1956)

Enrico Cerrachio contributed many pieces of sculpture to the Texas scene, including the famous equestrian statue of Sam Houston in Hermann Park at Houston, a bust of Governor Miriam A. Ferguson in the State Capitol, and a statue of President Anson Jones on the courthouse square at Anson in Jones County, Texas. The massive statue of Sam Houston, unveiled on August 12, 1925, towers above the pines in front of Miller Memorial. The Anson Jones Memorial consists of a seated bronze statue of heroic size, resting upon the second of two pink Marble Falls granite pedestals. A third block of polished granite serves as a background and bears an inscription.[5] Jones is dressed in a frock-coat, trousers, a single-breasted waistcoat, a fashionable neckcloth, and boots. He is studying a book which he holds in both hands. His face is lined with the wisdom of experience.

Cerrachio was born near Naples (Campania) in 1880. He studied at the Institute of Avelliono for three and one-half years under Rafael Bellezzo. He spent another two years learning to cast bronze and carve marble. He sailed to New York in 1900, and went to Houston in

[4] Giovanni Schiavo, *Four Centuries of Italian-American History.* (New York: Vigo, 1955), p. 238.

[5] Harold Schoen (et al.) *Monuments Erected By the State of Texas To Commemorate The Centenary of Texas Independence.* (Austin: Commission of Control For Texas Centennial Celebrations, 1938), p. 65.

1914. Soon he had commissions for a Doughboy statue, which the city presented to General John J. Pershing, and for busts of John Garner and Albert Einstein, as well as a statue of Rudolph Valentino.[6] One of Cerrachio's most interesting pieces was a bronze portrait head of Christ, two and one-half times life size. He displayed it in a velvet-lined case so designated and lighted that the head seemed to turn with the motion of the viewer, facing him directly at any angle. Cerrachio returned to New York City in 1944, and practiced his art there until his death in 1956.

ATTILIO AND FURIO PICCIRILLI

In 1888, two talented brothers, Attilio Piccirilli, and Furio Piccirilli, came to America to seek their fortunes. Attilio was born in Massa Carrara (Tuscany) in 1866, and Furio was born there two years later. The two men studied sculpture at the Accademia of San Luca in Rome. They worked together, and independently, to create numerous statues, medals, medallions, doors, friezes, and other sculptural pieces. Furio Piccirilli was elected an Associate Member of the National Academy. He won several awards, including honorable mention at the Pan-American Exposition, at Buffalo, New York, in 1901; a silver medal at the 1904 St. Louis Exposition; and another silver medal at the San Francisco Panama-Pacific Exposition in 1915.

Attilio Piccirilli was also an Associate Member of the National Academy. Between 1898 and his death in 1945, he sculptured numerous memorials and statues. Among them were the "MacDonough Monument" in New Orleans, the "Maine Memorial" in New York, "Dancing Faun" and "Head of Boy" located in the Buffalo Academy of Fine Arts.[7] Attilio designed and shaped

---

[6] Frances B. Fisk, *A History of Texas Artists and Sculptors*. (Abilene: Fisk, 1928), pp. 216-218.

[7] Mantle Fielding, *Dictionary of American Painters, Sculptors and Engravers*. (New York: Paul A. Struck, 1945), p. 283.

a magnificent monument to Richard Ellis on the courthouse square at Waxahachie, Texas. The seven foot, four
inch statue stands before a monolith of polished Texas
light pink granite.[8] Ellis is standing. He holds a copy of
the Texas Constitution in his left hand, and his right
hand is open, signaling sincerity. He is dressed in a large
frock-coat, trousers, cravat, and boots. The genius of
Piccirilli was his ability to portray detailed facial expressions, and the Ellis Memorial provides an excellent example of this ability. What a face! Proud and alert, will-
ful and intelligent.

The Piccirilli brothers worked together to carve a
memorial to "The Pioneer Woman," on the campus of
the Texas State College for Women (now the Texas
Woman's University). Donald Nelson designed the memorial, and Leo Friedlander designed the thirteen-foot
sculpture, which the Piccirilli brothers carved from a
thirty-ton monolith. The entire memorial is constructed
of Georgia white Cherokee marble and is axe-finished.
Above the ring base stands a great horizontal twenty-
two ton monolithic die with a bevelled top.[9] The Pioneer
Woman stands proudly erect, dressed in a long home-
spun cotton skirt, and matching jacket. Her left hand
rests upon the proximate collarbone, and her right hand
is extended downward. She seems determined and
stalwart-ready for anything which might confront her in
the pathless wilderness.

GAETANO CECERE

Gaetano Cecere, an Italian-American sculptor of
considerable talent, created two splendid statues in Texas. He was born of Italian parents in New York City in
1894, and held dual citizenship in Italy and the United
States. He was a pupil at the National Academy of Design, and received a scholarship in 1920 to study at the

[8] Schoen, *Monuments Erected By the State of Texas To Commemorate The Centenary of Texas Independence, op. cit.,* p. 59.
[9] *Ibid.,* p. 96.

American Academy in Rome. Cecere became an associate professor of art at Mary Washington College in Fredericksburg, Virginia, and he executed a number of reliefs for public buildings, including the United States Capitol. He is represented at the Norton Gallery in West Palm Beach, Florida, and at public buildings in Jacksonville, Florida, and Brookgreen Gardens, South Carolina.[10]

Cecere sculptured the "Sidney Sherman" monument at Galveston, and the "James Pinckney Henderson" monument at San Augustine. The memorial to Sidney Sherman is supported on a vast monolithic reinforced concrete foundation, upon which is set a offset platform of granite. The statue proper stands on a great horizontal die, in back of which stand three granite blocks. The center die contains an inscription. Above these three pieces is erected a seventeen foot monolithic die, forming a background for the statue. Upon this slab, directly back of the statue, is an intaglio design of Sherman mounted on his horse, raising his saber at the Battle of San Jacinto to cry "Remember the Alamo; Remember Goliad!" Another intaglio, symbolic of the relationship of Texas and the United States, appears on the back of the die. The memorial to James Pinckney Henderson rests on the courthouse grounds at San Augustine. It consists of two units; an outer ring capped with a granite curb, and the memorial proper, which consists of a square base of Marble Falls pink granite and a great hone-finished cylindrical die supporting the seated bronze portraiture.[11]

POMPEO COPPINI (1870-1957)

In 1901 the most important Italian sculptor to settle in Texas arrived in Austin. His name was Pompeo Coppini. The dazzling summit of human achievement repre-

---

[10] Bernard S. Myers, *McGraw-Hill Dictionary of Art.* Vol. I. New York: McGraw-Hill, 1969), p. 524.

[11] Schoen, *op. cit.,* pp. 58, 60.

SCULPTOR POMPEO COPPINI on a visit to San Antonio following the dedication of the Littlefield fountain in Austin. 30 March 1933.
— *Courtesy The San Antonio Light Collection,*
The University of Texas Institute of Texan Cultures,
at San Antonio, Texas

sented by this artist lasted a little more than forty years. But we must reckon the emergence of Coppini as one of the greatest events in the art history of the state. Monuments all over Texas recall his brilliance.

Coppini was born in Moglia (Tuscany) in 1870, and his family moved to Florence the following year. He studied under the best teachers of Europe, and graduated from the Academia di Belle Arti, Florence, with highest honors. In 1896, Coppini sailed to New York, where he eventually opened his own studio. He married in 1897, and became a naturalized American citizen in 1902. That year, he accepted a commission for the five statues which comprise the Confederate monument on the Capitol grounds at Austin. The sculptor liked San Antonio so well that he established a home and studio there, where the terrain and climate recalled his native region of Tuscany.

His next important work of art was an equestrian statue honoring Terry's Texas Rangers. He won the competition for the contract from no less eminent a colleague than Elizabet Ney. When the work was completed in 1907, it was widely acclaimed. Also in 1902, Coppini was commissioned to design a monument to President Rufus C. Burleson of Baylor. When the statue was completed, Mrs. Burleson declared that it looked exactly like the good doctor. In 1917, Coppini executed a similar memorial to Governor Sul Ross on the Texas A&M campus. The sculptor's name is doubtless remembered by several generations of freshmen who were annually required to clean the mud-daubed figure. The letters COPPINI, graved deeply in the base, left a lingering impression.

It took four years for Coppini to sculpt a marble statue of James P. Clarke for the Hall of Columns in the U.S. Capitol building at Washington, D.C. He completed the work in 1921.[12] The Italian also executed the monument at Sam Houston's tomb in Huntsville, the Texas heroes' memorial at Gonzales, a series of statues on The University of Texas at Austin campus, the Alamo cenotaph, and another series in the Hall of Texas Heroes at Dallas. He headed the art department at Trinity University in San Antonio from 1942 to 1945, when he returned to New York. Coppini died in 1957 and was buried in San Antonio.

The memorial to R. E. B. Baylor at Waco, on the campus of Baylor University, is a marvelous art work. It is supported on a continuous ring type footing, pier, and cap reinforced concrete foundation, designed as a rigid

---

[12] Forrester-O'Brien, *op. cit.*, pp. 250-253.

frame. The great platform is paved with a honed curb and axed slabs supporting five blocks of Marble Falls pink granite upon which is placed the seated bronze portraiture executed by Coppini. The sand-blown inscription appears on the rear block and two flanking blocks. Baylor is seated in the open Lincolnesque position, leaning slightly forward in an apparent gesture of interest.

The extraordinary Cenotaph Memorial at San Antonio has received worldwide acclaim. It was constructed of Georgia gray marble and rests upon a slab base of Texas pink granite. The great shaft rises sixty feet from its base forty feet in length and twelve feet in width. The theme of the monument is the Spirit of Sacrifice represented on the south and main face of the shaft by a magnificent idealistic figure rising twenty-three feet from the long sloping capstone emblematic of the tomb. This monolithic slab twenty feet long bears appropriate ornamental tracery. The east and west ledges are decorated with background panels of eight figures in low relief glorifying all of the men who died at the Alamo.

Before the east panel of the Alamo Cenotaph stand the heroic portrait statues of James Bowie and James Bonham; before the west panel, inspiring images of William Travis and David Crockett. On the north side appears a feminine figure symbolizing the state of Texas, holding the shields of Texas and the United States. Coppini conceived and carved the sculptural parts of the monument.[13] The Alamo Cenotaph passionately asserts the unity of man's body, mind, and spirit. It can be admired from the point of view of the body — those well formed figures of war heroes, and the beautiful feminine figure. It can also be looked at from the standpoint of the mind — a great embodiment of intellectual energy. But the awesome, rising idealistic effigy seems to imply that Coppini was chiefly concerned with the human spirit.

[13] Schoen, *op. cit.*, pp. 61, 84.

FORGOTTEN ITALIAN SCULPTORS

Two other Italian sculptors added to the art treasures of Texas. Their names were Ugo Lavaggi, and E. Leonarduzi. The author spent many hours examining Italian and American sources in an attempt to obtain information about them. To no avail. Still, their surnames are unquestionably Italian in origin, and this can easily be demonstrated by consulting any standard genealogical text. Ugo Lavaggi carved the "James Walker Fannin's Men" monument at Goliad State Park, and the "Rene Robert Cavelier De La Salle" memorial, located near Port Lavaca. Both works are beautifully proportioned *chefs-d'oeuvre* in pink granite. A handsome monument to "David Crockett," also in pink granite, by E. Leonarduzi, stands in the city square of Ozona, Texas.[14] The artist depicts Crockett as a man of great strength, and massive self-confidence.

OSCAR AND FREDERICK RUFFINI

Oscar and Frederick Ruffini were two of the finest architects to settle in Texas. Their works possess innovative style and conviction. One of the reasons why the architectural designs of the Ruffini brothers are so impressive is that the two men were also artists. Oscar painted a large watercolor of the Old Main Building which hangs in the Barker Texas History Center at the University of Texas at Austin. A number of drawings and watercolors by Frederick are on file in the Texas State Archives at Austin.[15] The collection of architectural works of the two brothers lists numerous banks, businesses, churches, county courthouses and jails, public buildings and schools, residences, and the Grape Creek Bridge.

---

[14] *Ibid.,* pp. 86, 104, 105.

[15] Texas State Archives, *Ruffini Collection, Architectural works of Oscar Ruffini and his brother, Frederick Ernest Ruffini,* Texas State Library, Austin, Texas, 20 pages.

FREDERICK ERNST RUFFINI, Architect of Old Main Building at University of Texas at Austin.
— *Courtesy Austin Public Library, Austin, Texas*
Copy From U.T. Institute of Texan Cultures,

Frederick Ruffini was born in Cleveland, Ohio, in 1851, of Genoese (Liguria) parents. He received his architectural training there and gained considerable experience before settling in Austin in 1877. Within four years he had designed a large number of private and public buildings such as the courthouses at Henderson, Longview, Georgetown, and Corsicana, jails at New Braunfels, McKinney, Franklin, and Groesbeck, and the old State Deaf and Dumb Asylum at Austin. Millets Opera House and the Hancock Building in Austin were also his handiwork. Ruffini's last project was his most imposing. In 1883, he was chosen as the architect, in an eight-entry competition, to design the Main Building for The University of Texas at Austin. In accordance with then fashionable trends, he chose Gothic frosting for the edifice, but he lived to see only the west wing completed. He died in 1885, during an epidemic which swept Austin.[16]

Oscar Ruffini was born in Cleveland, Ohio, on August 10, 1858. He received training as an architect in the Detroit office of Elijah E. Myers, the architect of the Texas State Capitol, and in the Austin office of his brother. By April 1884, he had gained enough experience to establish himself as an architect in San Angelo, the newly established county seat of Tom Green County. His first major commission was the San Angelo courthouse, the building which established his reputation. During his long career Oscar Ruffini designed numerous courthouses, schools, residences, and commercial buildings throughout West Texas. A collection of his architectural drawings, specifications, details, and watercolors of West Texas buildings are in the State Archives.[17] These include plans for the courthouses of Concho, Mills, Sutton, Sterling, and Crockett counties. He died on January 18, 1957, in San Angelo.

JOHN C. FILIPPONE

John C. Filippone was one of the greatest print makers in Texas. He was born in Brackettville, Texas, on July 26, 1894.[18] His father, Giovanni Battista Filippone, was born in Torino (Piedmont) on October 17, 1845. Giovanni arrived in New York on board the vessel *Queen,* on June 3, 1872, and by 1884 he had settled in Brackettville. He married a woman named Grace, and the couple had four children.[19]

[16] Roxanne Kuter Williamson, *Victorian Architecture in Austin.* (M.A. thesis, University of Texas at Austin, 1967), pp. 80-86.

[17] F. E. Ruffini and Oscar Ruffini Papers (MSS, Archives, Texas State Library, Austin).

[18] U.S. Government, Bureau of Immigration and Naturalization, *Petition For Naturalization,* Giovanni Battista Filippone, Washington, D.C., October 13, 1914.

[19] U.S. Government, Bureau of Immigration and Naturalization,

John C. Filippone demonstrated an aptitude for art early in his life. He studied art in St. Louis and New York and then made a grand tour of Italy, France, South America, Cuba, and Mexico, finally settling in San Antonio, Texas. John was one of the founders, and, for a number of years, a member of the Board of Directors of the Artists' Guild of San Antonio. He was awarded a gold medal and numerous honors for his extraordinary works in still life and portrait, Filippone's dry point etchings won him great popularity and acclaim.[20]

Among his many imaginative works are the beautiful, multicolored illustrations which appear in George Roe's version of *The Rubaiyat of Omar Khayyam*. In one print a Persian couple are seated underneath the bough of a tree, with one arm around each other's waist. There is a jug, a loaf of bread, some apples, and an open book of poems by their feet. The woman holds an ancient oriental lute in her left hand, while he offers her a small cup of wine. It is a picture of grown-up love, a marvelous amalgam of richness, tenderness, and trust, the richness symbolized by the ornate clothes worn by the couple, the tenderness by the hands, and the trust by the expression of the heads which, in their truth, have a spiritual glow.[21]

RODOLFO GUZZARDI (1903-1962)

Among the dozens of creative men and women who chose to elevate the glories of the Texas frontier, none was more singularly dedicated than the Italian-born painter Rodolfo Guzzardi. Guzzardi was born in Florence on April 15, 1903. He studied art in that city, and served a tour of duty in the Italian army. On January 6, 1921, Guzzardi became a journalist with the *Corriere della Laguna,* and he demonstrated considerable ability as a

Declaration of Intention, Giovanni Battista Filippone, Washington, D.C., November 19, 1913.

[20] Forrester-O'Brien, *op. cit.,* p. 307.

[21] George Roe, *The Rubaiyat of Omar Khayyam.* (Chicago: Laidlaw Bros., 1931), p. 31.

writer. But he was primarily a gifted painter with strong motivation to express his artistic talents. Guzzardi decided to go to the United States and attempt to capture the spirit of the American West, as Frederick Remington had done.

Guzzardi went to New York, where he met and married Josephine Doddis in 1933. The couple moved to Houston, and Rodolfo began to sketch Western scenes. Guzzardi quickly gained recognition for his work, and the Sacred Heart Dominican College of Houston offered him a teaching position in its Art Department, which he accepted. He later became the director of the department. He was described at that time as "very agile, with square shoulders and dark hair, mustache and 'mouche' " [22] Guzzardi died in 1962, but during his lifetime he created many extraordinary paintings. Giorgio Nicodemi commented on the artist's techniques, in his biography about Guzzardi. Nicodemi wrote: "The skill of execution is differently employed in the various works. Where the elements are portrayed from life, one can understand how every detail has been obtained with the control of the eye on the object, made with so much attention that one can perceive that every brush-stroke demanded a look and as the painting was born on the canvas or on the panel, the most varied thoughts were born and evoked the significance of what the painting was to be." [23]

Guzzardi's favorite subjects were landscapes and scenes depicting the rigors of the frontier life. He struggled toward an expression of art that was natural, and portrayed the simple, definite conditions of life. In his picture, "Palo Duro Canyon-Texas," Guzzardi strikingly reminds us of the duality of nature — the allure of gorgeous natural colors, contrasted with arid, barren, and desolate forms. How alone and insignificant the figures of the prospector and his mule seem in comparison to those tiresome expanses and serrated peaks. Another of his works,

[22] Giorgio Nicodemi, *Rodolfo Guzzardi*. (Milano: Ariel, 1952), p. 9.
[23] *Ibid.*, p. 16.

entitled "Galveston-Texas," contains vital splashes of colors which beautifully represent beach, water, sky, and clouds. Guzzardi's "Pioneer" is a meticulously drawn representation of a frontier home with every board and post depicted with great detail. This drawing is reminiscent of the work of the great Italian master, Canaletto. Guzzardi also produced a remarkable likeness of the "Mission of San Jose," located at San Antonio.

THE INFLUENCE OF ITALIAN ARCHITECTURAL STYLES IN TEXAS

In order to build edifices comparable to buildings in eastern cities, Texas leaders of the nineteenth century encouraged the use of Italianate architectural styles. They chose wisely. Beautiful Italian architectural designs date back to medieval and Renaissance times, when architects were artists. According to Kenneth Clark, Italian architects of that time had "given to their work a power of plastic invention, a sense of proportion and an articulation based on the study of the human figure, which knowledge of the tensile strength of steel, and other requisites of modern building, do not always produce." [24] The designs that were illustrated in Texas were adaptations of the street architecture of the Italian cities of Rome, Florence, and Venice. In the spirit of these illustrations, numerous commercial buildings appeared in Texas with Florentine or Venetian arches, brackets, heavy cornices, and pilasters with Classical orders. By the 1860s Galveston had three- and four-story buildings in the mode along the famous Strand and along Tremont Street, and during the 1870s and 1880s this fashionable style spread to other business centers of the state.

Many of the county courthouses built in Texas during the 1880s derived their architectural style from Italy. For example, the Lampasas County Courthouse in

[24] Kenneth Clark, *Civilisation.* (New York: Harper & Row, 1969), p. 171.

Lampasas (1883), with its rusticated cut-stone quoins and decorative consoles, typified the beauty of the Italianate mode. Other examples were the Stephens County Courthouse in Breckenridge (1883) and the Shackelford County Courthouse in Albany (1883). Another example with projecting pavilions in the Italianate was the Hood County Courthouse (1889-1891) in Granbury, similar to the one in Lampasas. This Italianate trend remained popular in Texas until the early 1890s.[25]

CONCLUSION

Italian artists were atypical of the Italian experience in Texas. These artists were individualistic, cosmopolitan, and internationally minded. With their talents to sustain them, they could have succeeded in almost any civilized area. But the challenge of capturing and preserving on canvas or granite the confidence and vitality of a dynamic frontier people was a powerful allure. Italian artists were also inspired to come to Texas by the magnificent natural landscapes and seascapes available there. They contributed greatly to the art treasures of Texas.

[25] Willard B. Robinson (et al.), *Texas Public Buildings of the Nineteenth Century.* (Austin: University of Texas Press, 1974), pp. 197-201.

ITALIAN TEXANA

Folklore — traditional customs, beliefs, tales, or sayings preserved unreflectively among a people

The Italian settlers in Texas had a folklore all their own. This folklore was derived from the regional and local cultures from which they came. Remnants of the Italian folk culture remain in the form of fairy tales, legends, stories and jests, proverbs and family recipes and folk dances. Scores of taped interviews have provided access to the folk history of Italian Texans whose heritage might otherwise be lost. This is particularly true of the *contadini* which had a predominantly oral rather than a written tradition. Except for family recipes which were written and handed down from generation to generation, the folk culture described in this chapter is given exactly as it was taken from the mouths of the Italian Texans who were interviewed. However, the author has taken the liberty of adding grammatical corrections whenever they did not interfere with the richness of the materials. He has also provided the Italian translation for the proverbs, which for the most part, were remembered only in English.

THE SICILIAN FARMERS
OF BRYAN AND DICKINSON

In the shade of the huge cone of Etna, the Sicilian triangle offers the extreme variety of its coastal and mountain scenery, as well as a wealth of fascinating features left by its age-old cultural and social history. Between 1881 and 1901 the population of the island increased at a rate of 20.5 percent. The average density was extremely high for a region which lived almost exclusively by agriculture, and was much higher than the average for Italy in general. In 1905 the population was 3,568,124. The Sicilian *contadini* who migrated to Texas came from three small farming communities near Palermo.

THE THIRTEENTH: A SICILIAN FAIRY TALE

There was once a father who had thirteen sons, the youngest of whom was named Thirteenth. It was difficult for the father to support his children, but he earned what he could gathering herbs. To inspire her children, the mother said to them: "The one among you who comes home first each day will have herb soup." Thirteenth usually returned home first and ate the soup, and thereby incurred the envy of his brothers.

A hideous ogre menaced the land where the family lived. The king of that region issued a proclamation that whoever was brave enough to steal the ogre's bedspread would be rewarded with gold. Thirteenth's brothers went to the king and said: "Majesty, we have a brother, named Thirteenth, who is confident that he can steal the bedspread." The king ordered: "Bring him to me at once." They brought Thirteenth to the king. The unfortunate subject asked: "Majesty, how will it be possible for me to steal the ogre's bedspread? If he sees me he will eat me!" "No matter, you must go," ordered the king. "I

[1] There are several versions of the fairy tales described in this chapter. For the actual Italian version consult:

    a. *The Thirteenth* — Giuseppe Pitre, *La Scatola di Cristallo. Novellina popolare senese raccolta da Giuseppe Pitre* (Palermo, Montuoro-Di Giovanni, 1875).

    b. *In Love With a Statue* — Domenico Comparetti, *Novelline popolari italiene pubblicate ed illustrate da Domenico Comparetti*. Vol. I. (Turin: A. D'Ancona, 1875).

    c. *The Cobbler* — *Novella ja fiorentina, El Sciavattin,* Milano.

know that you are bold, and this act of bravery must be performed." Thirteenth departed and went to the house of the ogre, who was not at home. But the ogress was in the kitchen. Thirteenth entered quietly and hid himself under the bed. At night the ogre returned. He ate his supper and went to bed saying: "I smell human flesh. When I discover it I shall eat it!" The ogress replied: "Be still; no one has entered here." The ogre fell asleep and began to snore, and Thirteenth pulled the bedspread a little. The ogre awoke and exclaimed: "What is that?" Thirteenth began to mew like a cat. The ogress said: "Scat! scat!" and clapped her hands, and then fell asleep again with the ogre. Then Thirteenth gave a hard pull, seized the bedspread, and ran away. The ogre heard him running, recognized him in the dark, and said: "I know you! You are Thirteenth."

After a time the king issued a second proclamation, that whoever would steal the ogre's horse and bring it to the king would receive an even larger measure of gold. Filled with confidence, Thirteenth again presented himself, and asked for a silk ladder and a bag of cakes. He departed with these things, and at night went to the ogre's house. He climbed up the wall surrounding the house without being heard, and descended to the stable. The horse neighed on seeing him, but he offered it a cake. He mounted it, kept feeding it the cakes, and brought it to the king's stable.

The king issued a third proclamation, that he would give a very large measure of gold to whoever would bring him the ogre's pillow. Thirteenth said: "Majesty, how is that possible? The pillow is full of little bells, and you must know that the ogre awakens at a breath." "I know nothing about that," bellowed the king. "I wish it at any cost." Thirteenth departed, and went and crept under the ogre's bed. At midnight he stretched out his hand very gently, but the little bells sounded. "What was that?" asked the ogre? "Nothing," replied the ogress; "perhaps it was the wind that made them ring." But the suspicious ogre pretended to sleep, and kept his ears alert. Thirteenth stretched out his hand again. Alas! the ogre seized his arm. "Now you are caught! I will make you suffer for the things you have stolen from me." He locked Thirteenth in a large barrel, and began to feed him raisins and figs. After a time he said: "Stick out your finger, little Thirteenth, so I can see whether you are fat." Thirteenth stuck out the tail of a mouse, who was sharing the barrel with him. "Ah, how thin you are! said the ogre; "and besides, you don't smell good! Eat, my son; take the raisins and figs, and get fat soon!" After some days the ogre told him again to put out his finger, and Thirteenth stuck out a spindle. "Eh, wretch! are you still lean? Eat, eat, and get fat soon."

At the end of a month Thirteenth had nothing more to stick out, and was obliged to show his finger. The ogre cried out in joy: "He is fat, he is fat!" The ogress hastened to the spot: "Quick my ogress, heat the oven three nights and three days, for I am going to invite our relatives, and we will make a fine banquet of Thirteenth."

The ogress heated the oven three days and three nights, and then released Thirteenth from the barrel, and said to him: "Come here, Thirteenth; you must help me to put a large lamb in the oven." But Thirteenth was wise to her deception; and when he approached the oven he said: "Ah, mother ogress, what is that black thing in the corner of the oven?" The ogress stooped down a little, but saw nothing. "Stoop down again," said Thirteenth, "so that you can see it." When she stooped down again, her round, extended posterior and full figure convinced Thirteenth that the ogress would make a finer meal than him. He seized her by the feet and threw her into the oven, and then closed the oven door. Thirteenth ran away to the king with the pillow and the ogre's most valuable things.

After this, the king said to Thirteenth: "Listen, Thirteenth. To complete your valiant exploits, I wish you to bring me the ogre himself, in person, alive and well."

"How can I, your Majesty?" asked Thirteenth. Then he roused himself, and added: "I see how, now!" Then he had a very strong chest made, and disguised himself as a monk, with a long, false beard, and went to the ogre's house, and called out to him: "Do you know Thirteenth? The wretch! He has killed our superior; but if I catch him! If I catch him, I will shut him up in this chest!" At these words the ogre drew near and said: "I, too, would like to help you, against that wretch of an assassin, for you don't know what he has done to me." And he began to tell his story. "But what shall we do?" asked the pretended monk. "I do not know Thirteenth. Do you know him?" "Yes, sir." "Then tell me, father ogre, how tall is he?" "As tall as I am." "If that is so," said Thirteenth, "Let us see whether this chest will hold you; if it will hold you, it will hold him." "Oh, good!" said the ogre; and he got into the chest. Then Thirteenth shut the chest and said: "Look carefully, father ogre, and see whether there is any hole in the chest." "There is none." "Just wait; let us see whether it shuts well, and is heavy to carry."

Meanwhile Thirteenth shut and nailed up the chest, took it on his back, and hurried to the city. When the ogre cried out: "Enough now!" Thirteenth ran all the faster, and, laughing, sang this song to taunt the ogre:

"I am Thirteenth,
Who carry you on my back;
I have tricked you and am going to trick you.
I must deliver you to the king."

When he reached the castle, the king had an iron chain attached to the ogre's hands and feet. The king gave Thirteenth great riches and treasures, and always desired him at his side, as a man of the highest valor.

SICILIAN PROVERBS, ADMONITIONS, AND PICTURESQUE EXPRESSIONS

A chi fa male, mai mancano scuse. — The wrongdoer never lacks excuses.

Chi non fa, non falla. — The man who does nothing makes no mistakes.

Le disgrazie non vengon mai sole. — Misfortunes never come singly.

Lontan dagli occhi, lontan dal cuore. — Out of sight, out of mind.

Meglio un uovo oggi che una gallina domani. — Better an egg today than a chicken tomorrow.

Il mondo e di chi ha pazienza. — The world belongs to the man who is patient.

Non ogni fiore fa buon odore. — Not every flower has a sweet odor.

Pietra mossa non fa muschio. — A rolling stone gathers no moss.

Presto maturo, presto marcio. — The sooner ripe, the sooner rotten.

Sdegno d'amante poco dura. — A lover's indignation does not last long.

SICILIAN RECIPES

Stuffed Artichokes Agrigento Style

12 artichokes
Filling:
  3 ounces fillets desalted
    anchovy, chopped
  2 ounces salame, chopped
  1 tablespoon grated
    Pecorino
  1 clove garlic, chopped

1 tablespoon chopped parsley
3 tablespoons bread crumbs,
  soaked in oil and lemon
  juice
Salt and pepper
Oil
Juice of 2 lemons

Trim, remove hard outer leaves and choke, and wash the artichokes; reserve in water acidified with a little lemon juice. Prepare the filling by combining the anchovy, salame, Pecorino, garlic, and parsley well with the bread crumbs, seasoning with salt and pepper. When required, drain and dry the artichokes, and, with a spoon, open up the centers and stuff them with the prepared filling, adding plenty of oil and lemon juice. Transfer the artichokes to an oiled pan and pour in sufficient cold water to half cover them; season with salt and pepper. Put the pan into a moderate oven for one hour, basting frequently. Transfer to a serving dish, pouring over the pan juices. Serves 6.

Stuffed Cannoli

Dough:
2 cups flour, sifted
  strong red wine
1 tablespoon sugar
  Pinch salt
Fat for deep-frying
Filling:

½ pound very fresh ricotta
½ cup confectioner' sugar
  Pinch of salt
1 tablespoon pistachio nuts,
  sliced lengthwise
2 tablespoons finely
  chopped candied fruit
Chopped pine nuts

Dough: Make a mound of the flour on a tabletop; scoop out the center and mix in the wine, the sugar, and the salt. Knead until a firm dough is obtained. Roll it into a ball, wrap it in a slightly damp cloth, and allow to rest for two hours. Then roll it out into sheets of about 1/16 of an inch thick; cut into 5-inch squares and roll around the special cannoli metal tubes (any metal tubes 5 inches long and 1 inch in diameter will do). When all the cannoli have been prepared, heat plenty of oil for deep-frying. Put the cannoli in a few at a time and remove them when golden brown. Drain, cool, and reserve. As the cannoli cool, the metal tubes can be carefully removed.

To fill: Put the ricotta, sugar and salt in a mixing bowl or blender. Mix well until smooth and pass through a fine sieve. Then combine with the pistachio nuts and candied fruit. Using a pastry bag with an open nozzle, fill the tubes with the filling; sprinkle the chopped pine nuts over the filling at the extremities of the cannoli. Makes 12-15.

THE PIEDMONTESE FARMERS
OF MONTAGUE COUNTY

From Turin to Milan in the great plains furrowed by the Po River and on the splendid shores of Lake Maggiore and Lake Como, we find cities, abbeys and castles of ancient civilizations, world-famous names and towns. Physically, the Region of Piedmont is the upper gathering-ground and valley of the Po River, enclosed on all the sides except towards the Lombard plain by a vast semicircle of the Alps. At the turn of the century, the people were chiefly engaged in agriculture, in the reeling and throwing of silk, and in the manufacture of cotton, woolens and clothing. The Piedmontese who migrated to Montague County came primarily from villages in Turin Province.

IN LOVE WITH A STATUE:
A PIEDMONTESE FAIRY TALE

There was once a king who had two sons. The eldest son did not wish to marry, and the youngest, although he travelled extensively, found no lady to meet his high standards. While travelling he discovered a beautiful marble statue of a voluptuous lady and fell in love with it. He bought it, had it delivered to his room, and every day he embraced and kissed it. One day his father became aware of this, and told his son: "What are you doing? If you want a wife, take one of flesh and bones, and not one of marble." The son responded that he would marry a woman exactly like the statue, or not marry at all. His older brother went out into the world in a quest to find the special woman represented by the statue. On his journey he met a man who owned an extraordinary mouse which could dance like a human being. He said to himself: "I shall take it home to my brother to amuse himself with." He continued his quest, and, arrived at a distant town, where he found a bird that sang like an angel, and purchased that, too, for his brother. He was about to return home, when he saw a beggar knocking at a door. A very beautiful girl appeared at the window, who resembled in every respect the prince's statue. Suddenly, she withdrew. The brother told the beggar to ask for alms again; but he refused, because he feared that the magician who lived there would return home and cast a spell on him. But the prince offered the beggar so much money that he knocked again. The young girl reappeared, and suddenly withdrew. The prince conceived of a plan. He went through the streets, proclaiming that he mended and sold looking-glasses. The servant of the young girl, who heard him, told her mistress to go and see the mirrors. She went, and he enticed her aboard his ship by telling her of some extraordinary selections that he had there. Then he set sail as she wept and decried his actions.

Upon returning home the magician sent out a magical black bird to seek vengeance against the abductor of his daughter. At sea, the prince and lady heard the voice of the bird, saying: "What a handsome mouse you have! You will take it to your brother; you will turn his head; and if you tell him of it, you will become marble. A fine bird you have; you will take it to your brother; you will turn his head; and if you tell him, you will become marble. A fine lady you have; you will take her to your brother; you will turn his head; and if you tell him of it, you will become marble." Fearing for his life, the elder brother decided to remain silent. They landed, and the prince took the mouse to his brother; and when he had seen it and wanted it, he cut off its head. Then he showed him the bird that sang like an angel, and his brother wanted it; but the elder brother also cut off its head.

Then he said: "I have something handsomer," and he produced the beautiful girl who looked like the statue. and the brother who had brought her said nothing, and the other feared that he would take her away from him too. The younger brother had the elder thrown into prison, where he continued to remain silent. Because of this, he was condemned to die. Three days before his sentence was to be carried out, he asked his brother to visit him in prison. Then the condemned brother said: "A large black bird told me that if I brought you back the dancing mouse, and spoke, I should become a statue." And saying this, he became a statue to the waist. "And if, bringing you the singing bird, I spoke, it would be the same." Then he became a statue to his chest. "And if, bringing you the lady, I spoke, I should become a statue." Then he became a statue all over, and his brother began to lament in despair, and tried in vain to restore him to life. All kinds of physicians came, to no avail. Finally there came one who said that he was capable of restoring life to the prince provided that his terms were met. The king agreed, and the physician demanded the blood of the king's two youngest children. The Queen refused to consent. Then the king gave a ball, and while his wife was dancing he had the two children killed, and ordered that the statue of the prince be bathed with their blood. The prince was restored to life. After becoming aware of the treachery, the Queen ran to her children and found them half dead. She fainted. All around her sought to console the Queen; but when she opened her eyes and saw the physician smiling, she cried: "Out of my sight, ugly wretch! It was you who caused my children to be murdered." He replied: "Pardon me, my lady, I have done no harm. go and see whether your children are there!" She ran to see, and found them alive and at play. Then the physician said: "I am the magician, your father, whom you forsook, and I have wished to show you what it is to love one's children." Then they made peace, and remained happy and contented.

NORTHERN ITALIAN PROVERBS, ADMONITIONS, AND PICTURESQUE EXPRESSIONS

A chi vuole non mancano modi. — Where there's a will, there's a way.

Al bisogno si conosce un amico. — A friend is known in time of need.

Amor regge senza legge. — Love rules without rules.

Chi non s'arrischia non guadagna. — Who risks nothing gains nothing.

[2] The Italian proverbs were taken from too many sources to cite. However, the following two books: *The Merriam-Webster Dictionary of Foreign Phrases and Abbreviations;* C.O. Sylvester Mawson, *Dictionary of Foreign Terms.* (New York: Thomas Crowell, 1975); contain many of them.

Chi parla troppo non puo parlar sempre bene. — He who speaks too much cannot always speak well.

Chi va piano va sano; chi va sano va lontano. — He who goes softly goes safely; he who goes safely goes far.

Dove l'oro parla, ogni lingua tace. — Where gold speaks, every tongue is silent.

E buon orator chi a se persuade. — It is a good orator who convinces himself.

E meglio un buon amico che cento parenti. — Better one good friend than a hundred relatives.

Fatti maschii, parole femine. — Deeds are males, words females.

PIEDMONTESE RECIPES

Salmon Braised in Barolo Wine

3½ pound salmon
3 pints fish fumet
Sauce:
  1 small onion, chopped
  1 small carrot, chopped
  1 celery stalk, chopped
  5 tablespoons of butter
  2 tablespoons oil
  3 cups of Barolo wine

24 stalks fresh mushrooms
Salt and pepper
2 tablespoons butter mixed with 1½ tablespoons flour
24 caps fresh mushrooms, cleaned and simmered in butter, salt, and a little water until cooked and firm

Clean and prepare the salmon and place in a deep pan; cover with fish fumet and simmer for about 20 minutes. Pour half of the fumet into another pan and reduce it by half; strain through a damp cheesecloth and reserve.

Sauce: Fry the onion, carrot, and celery in 1½ tablespoons of butter and 2 tablespoons of oil; drain off the fat and add the wine and mushroom stalks. Season with a little salt and pepper and simmer for 20 minutes. Pass through a fine sieve. Then heat the butter and flour paste and pour in to thicken the

[3] *Sicilian Recipes* — courtesy of Josephina Marie Liggio, 4124 Liggio Street, Dickinson, Texas.

Piedmontese Recipes — courtesy of Delfina Carminati, Box 157, Montague, Texas.

Northern Italian Recipes — courtesy of Lorenzo Santi, 8955 Long Point, Houston, Texas.

sauce. Add the remaining 3½ tablespoons of butter and the fish fumet, mixing well with an egg whisk. Drain the salmon and remove its skin from head to tail. Place on a serving dish, cover with sauce, surround with cooked mushroom caps, and serve hot. Serves 6 to 8.

Piedmontese Risotto

2 ounces salt pork, minced
1 tablespoon chopped onion
¼ pound butter
A mixture of:
1 small carrot, grated
1 celery stalk, chopped
2 sprigs parsley, chopped
4 slices Italian salami chopped

¼ pound chicken livers and hearts, sliced
1 pound large-grain rice
4 cups chicken stock
Salt and pepper
1 cup grated Parmesan cheese

In a deep saucepan, large enough to hold the rice, fry the salt pork and onion in half the butter. When the onion is golden in color add the carrot, celery, and parsley mixture. Cook for a few minutes and add the salami, chicken livers and hearts. Continue cooking the mixture for about 10 minutes on a moderate heat, then add the rice. Stir for a minute or two and pour in 1 cup of stock, stirring constantly. When the rice has absorbed the stock, add another cup and so on until the stock has been used. Cover the pot and cook over a slow heat for about 20 minutes, checking occasionally to see if more liquid is required. Add salt and pepper to taste. At the end of the cooking, add the rest of the butter and 2 tablespoons of cheese; mix well, cover again, remove from heat and leave the risotto to rest for a few minutes. Put into a heated serving bowl and sprinkle a tablespoon of grated cheese on top. The remaining cheese is served at the table. Serves 6.

THE NORTHERN ITALIANS OF ERATH AND VICTORIA COUNTIES

After visiting the splendid villas along the banks of the Brenta River and stopping at Padua and Rovigo, it is possible to see the more important towns in Emilia and some delightful Renaissance Capitals. Emilia is a territorial division of Italy, bounded by Venetia and Lombardy on the north. Modena is one of the principal cities of Emilia. Modenese laborers worked the rich coal mines of thurber, as did Venetians and Piedmontese. At the turn of the century commerce in Modena was chiefly agricultural and was stimulated by a good position in the railway system, and by a canal which opened a waterway by the Panaro and the Po to the Adriatic. In Venetia the principal crops were wheat, rice, grapes, mulberry leaves, tobacco, chestnuts, potatoes and hemp. It is not surprising that Italian railroad workers from Lombardy helped to build the rail line from Victoria to Rosenberg. Milan, the chief city, was the greatest railway center in Italy. It was in direct communication with the principal towns of Lombardy, the rest of Italy, and with the larger towns of France, Germany and Switzerland. Other railroad centers in the region included Mortara, Pavia, and Mantua. Because of the relative flatness of Lombardy, every large town was situated on or within easy reach of the railway.

THE COBBLER: A MILANESE FAIRY TALE

There was once a cobbler who one day was so tired of cobbling that he said: "Now I will go and seek my fortune." He bought a little cheese and put it on the table. It got full of flies, and he took an old shoe, and hit the cheese and killed all the flies. He afterward counted them, and noted that five hundred were dead, and four hundred wounded. He then girded on a sword, and put on a cocked hat, and went to the court, and said to the king: "I am the chief warrior of the flies. Five hundred I have killed, and four hundred I have wounded." The king responded: "Since you are a warrior, you will be brave enough to climb that mountain there, where there are two magicians, and kill them. If you kill them, you shall marry my daughter." Then he gave him a white flag to wave when he had killed them. "And sound the trumpet, you will put his head in a bag, both the heads, to show me."

The cobbler then departed, and found a house, which was an inn, and the innkeeper and his wife were none other than the magician and his wife. He asked for lodging and food, and all he needed. Afterward he went to his room; but before going to bed, he looked up at the ceiling. He saw a great stone over the bed. Warily, instead of getting into bed, he slept in a corner of the room. When a certain hour struck, the magicians let the stone drop and it crushed the whole bed. The next morning the cobbler went down and complained that he could not sleep because of the noise. They told him that they would change his room. That evening, the same thing happened, and in the morning they told him they would give him another room. When it was a certain hour, the husband and wife went to the forest to cut a bundle of sticks. Then when the magician went home; the cobbler with a sickle in his hand, said: "Wait until I help you to take the bundle off your back." Then he gave the magician a blow with the sickle and cut off his head. He did the same thing when the magician's wife returned. Then he unfurled his flag, and sounded his trumpet, and a band went out to meet him. After he had arrived at the court, the king said to him: "Now that you have killed the two magicians, you will marry my daughter." But the cobbler had got so used to drawing the thread that he did so in his sleep, and kept hitting his wife on the derriere, which was quite reddened every morning. His wife was, of course, an absolute fox — bad enough to warrant a daily spanking! However, she could not rest, and lost a considerable amount of weight, and therefore complained to her father. Then the king gave the cobbler a great deal of money and sent him home.

NORTHERN ITALIAN PROVERBS, ADMONITIONS, AND PICTURESQUE EXPRESSIONS

Gli assenti hanno torto. — The absent are always in the wrong.

Guerra cominciata, inferno scatenato. — War commenced, hell unchained.

I frutti proibiti sono i piu dolci. — Forbidden fruits are the sweetest.

Il volto sciolto ed i pensieri stretti. — The countenance open, but the thoughts withheld.

I pazzi per lettera sono i maggiori pazzi. — Learned fools are the biggest fools.

Mille verisimili non fanno un vero. — A thousand probabilities do not make one truth.

Non si puo far d'un pruno, un melarancio. — You cannot make an orange tree out of a bramble bush.

Ogni cane e leone a casa sua. — Every dog is a lion at home.

Ogni vero non e buono a dire. — Every truth is not good to be told.

Pensa molto, parla poco, e scrivi meno. — Think much, speak little, and write less.

NORTHERN ITALIAN RECIPES

Veal Piccata (Lombardy)

1½ pounds veal, fillet
2 ounces prosciutto
Salt and pepper
1½ tablespoons chopped parsley

Flour
½ cup butter
1 lemon

Cut the veal into thin 1-ounce slices, all of equal size and shape. Cut the prosciutto into thin strips. Pound the veal lightly and season with a little salt and pepper, then dust in flour. Heat 6 tablespoons of butter in a pan and add the veal slices; turn up the heat a little and saute the slices on both sides till golden. Transfer to a warmed serving dish. Add the remaining butter to the pan juices, add the ham strips and when the ham begins to color, add a squeeze of lemon juice. Pour the pan juices over the piccata slices and sprinkle chopped parsley over all. Serve very hot. Serves 6.

Shrimp Hors D'oeuvres (Emilia-Romagna)

24 very large shrimps	1 tablespoon oil
4 lettuce leaves	1 teaspoon vinegar
4 hard-boiled eggs	Pinch of salt
1 cup mayonnaise	Pinch of pepper

Clean, devein, shell, and cook the shrimps; chop the shrimp meat. Prepare individual plates, each with a lettuce leaf, on which the shrimp meat is distributed, surrounded by wedges of hard-boiled eggs. Prepare mayonnaise, combine into a little oil, vinegar, salt, and a grinding of fresh pepper; distribute over each dish. Serves 4.

Mussels in the Pan (Venetian)

3 pounds mussels	
½ cup of oil	2 tablespoons vinegar
A mixture of:	Salt and pepper
3 garlic cloves, chopped	
3 tablespoons chopped parsley	
2 tablespoons bread crumbs	

Scrub and beard the mussels and wash them in water; put 2 tablespoons oil in a pan along with the mussels and saute them over a brisk heat until the shells open. Then remove them from the stove; discard the empty shells and remove the top shell from each. Lay the bottom shells, with the mussels in them, in a pan and distribute over each a pinch of the garlic, parsley, bread-crumb mixture. Combine the remaining oil with 2 tablespoons of vinegar and sprinkle over all, seasoning also with salt and pepper. Preheat a moderate oven and put the pan in it; remove when the bread crumbs begin to brown. Serves 6.

ITALIAN FOLK MUSIC

Folk music was part of the culture of early Italian Texans. This is not surprising. Italy is famous for its many colorful folk dances. Generally these dances are careless in rhythm, noisy and exuberant, accompanied by clapping, stamping, heel tapping and whistling. In some there is tense, neat movement with outbursts of pantomine relying on literal stories and the acting out re-

THE TARANTELLA was danced by couples in Sicily at the turn of the century.

lationships among people. Both pantomine and farce are popular.

The Tarantella is perhaps the most widely known Italian folk dance. It is especially popular in southern Italy, although the dance has adherents all over the country. The quality of movement of the dance is frenzied. It is gay, animated, and usually concerned with guessing how many fingers can be seen in a suddenly opened hand. Traditionally, it does not have a set pattern, but is composed of a number of figures irregularly arranged to suit the mood of the dancers.

The Tarantella antedates recorded history. The movements of the dance are depicted on ancient Greek vases, and drawings on the walls of the ruins of Pompeii, indicating that it was well known by the Romans. A popular legend has it that the Tarantella comes from the jumping that doctors once prescribed for people bitten by the Tarantula, a kind of wolf spider that thrives in southern Italy. The legend perpetuated a myth that the bite of the spider is fatal to its victims, and that the only cure lay in rapid exercise in order to sweat out the poison. It is now known that although the bite of the Tarantula is painful and produces some swelling, it almost never causes death or severe debilitation. There was considerable discussion on this topic at the Venice Congress and Folk Festival in September 1949. The consensus of opinion was that the dance had no relation to the bite of the spider, and that this misconception may have arisen from the similarity of names. The dance may have acquired its name from the town of Taranto, in Southern Italy.

There is another legend regarding the Tarantella of Sorrento — the Sorrentina. The story involves Sirens — sea nymphs, who lured sailors with their sweet songs to shipwreck on the rocky coast. According to Homer, Ulysses' ship sailed into the waters of the Sirens, but he escaped the danger of their fatal songs by having his men tie him to the mast after stopping their ears with

VALENTINO and IRMA BELFIGLIO prepare to dance The
Tarantella at the 1982 Dallas International Bazaar.

wax. Angered and frustrated by the guile of Ulysses, the
Sirens asked the daughters of Zeus to teach them something that could help defeat the King of Ithaca through
his eyesight. In response, the Greek goddesses created
the Sorrentina, which, alas, the sea nymphs could not
dance, since they were mermaids, and had no legs. Nevertheless, the girls of Sorrento and Capri learned the gay
and graceful dance.

The Tarantella appears with its present name only in
the last four or five centuries. In earlier times it was referred to as Lucia, Sfessania, Villanella and other names.
The Tarantella underwent some changes and acquired
the use of castanets when it was fused with the Fandango. The Fandango is a Spanish dance in tripple time
which appeared in Southern Italy when it was dominated by the Spanish in the fifteenth century.

There is an interesting reference to the Tarantella in
an almanac of the year 1891, which is reported by Anton

Guilio Bragaglia in his article in the December 1949 issue of *Ricreazione.* It says: "Let us take ourselves to Italy, to this cradle of choreography and of all the arts. To the sound of castanets and of tambourines and to the music of mandolins the vivacious Tarantella jumps and designs voluptuous movements in Taranto and in Calabria and also in Le Puglie and in Naples. Its setups and its evolutions, the pauses of the two dancers dramatize flirtation, jealousy, disdain, pleasure, regret, all the expressions of that great poem of the heart which is called love!"

The Sicilian people who settled in Texas loved gaiety and mimicry. Every festivity, public or private, was a pretext to get a group of friends together. They often rapidly improvised an orchestra, and danced the Tarantella at home or in some public place. At weddings in Bryan, Hearne and Dickinson, the Tarantella was part of the ceremony, for when the bride was taken to the groom's house, together with her many gifts and trousseau, the guests immediately danced the Tarantella in honor of the newlyweds.

The Sicilian Tarantella is full of movement and abandon, expressing the joy of being alive. Yet its actions and movements are never immodest, for that would not be tolerated by the chaste habits of "La Conca d'Oro," the golden basin, so-called because of the many orange groves which abound in the region. The Sicilians do not generally use castanet or tambourines while dancing. Their sole accompaniment is the rhythmic beating of the hands. The Tarantella is still danced today by Italian Texans during some festivals, weddings and holidays. In the Spring of 1982 a troupe from the Italian Club of Dallas danced the Tarantella at the Dallas International Bazaar to the delight of Dallasites.

CONCLUSION

THE WINDS OF CHANGE

Dead dreams of days forsaken,
Blind buds that snows have shaken
Wild leaves that winds have taken. —
Algernon C. Swinburne,
The Garden of Proserpine.

The graveyard at Montague appears to be under some dread enchantment. In winter, chilling winds swirl around the gray tombstones, disturbing the Texas wintergrass and scrubby blackjack oak trees. In summer, the hot blazing sun bakes the land. Dead men and dead women lie under stone epitaphs there — the remains of the original Italian settlers. But what of their descendants? Wedding receptions without folk music, evening meals without wine, Sunday afternoons spent watching the Dallas Cowboys, and Texas drawls. These behaviors are shared similarly by Italian Americans, and many other ethnic groups living in Texas today. Paradoxically, Italian clubs currently flourish in Texas. A few examples are: The Italian Club of Dallas, The Italy in America Association of Houston, The Christopher Columbus Italian Society of San Antonio, and the American Italian Association of El Paso. These clubs host Italian cultural events, festivals, dinners, wine-tastings, bocce tournaments, and symposiums. They also sponsor inexpensive Italian language classes, charter tours to Italy, and engage in charitable and civic affairs, and mutual aid pro-

VINCENZO E. DE NARDO, Associate Professor of Italian at Southern Methodist University, received his Ph.D. from the University of California at Los Angeles and a Doctor's Degree in Jurisprudence from the University of Rome. He is a contributor to Italian and American journals.

MR. & MRS. ADAM E. JANELLI ca. 1890 (He brought the Salvation Army to Texas in 1889)

— Courtesy Mrs. E. T. Crosson, Dallas, Texas
Copy From U.T. Institute of Texan Cultures,
San Antonio, Texas

COUNT and COUNTESS ROBERTO AGOSTINI are relatively new arrivals in Texas. Born in Venice, the Count is now in charge of the International Division of the Southern Metals Corporation of Dallas.

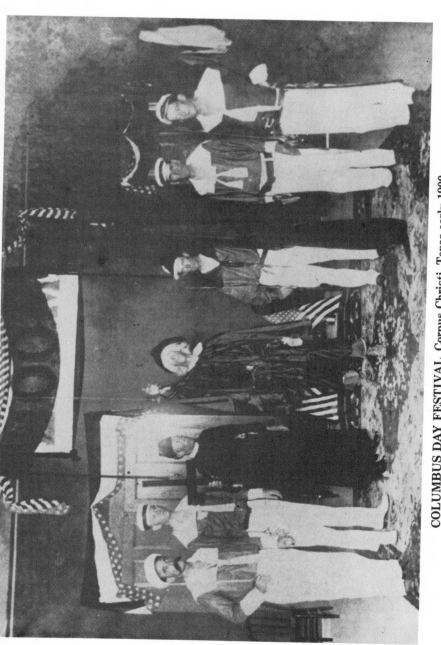

COLUMBUS DAY FESTIVAL. Corpus Christi, Texas early 1900s
— *Courtesy La Retama Library*
Corpus Christi, Texas

grams. Together in 1980, they raised thousands of dollars in aid for Italian earthquake victims.

What is the nature of the corporate will that seeks to preserve Italianism by institutionalizing it in the form of Italian clubs? This study will attempt to isolate and identify distinguishing cultural traits which appear to be common among Italian Americans of different generations. Because the American society places a premium on conformity and mobility, assimilationist pressures have been strong, and the maintenance of group identity has been very difficult. Three broad concepts of assimilation have emerged in this century, and new theories are currently being advanced. The "melting pot" theory suggests the desirability and inevitability of biological and cultural amalgamation,[1] whereas, some writers advocate separation and segregation,[2] as ways of strengthening group life, bolstering individual identity and psychological wholeness, and furthering group interests in a competitive multicultural society. "Cultural pluralism" is an attempt to live in both worlds at the same time in order to take advantage of primary group associations for personal, familial, and cultural needs, while utilizing secondary group contacts in the civic, economic, and political environments.[3]

Assimilation and acculturation also have been the subject of differing theories about the predicted decline or resurgence of ethnicity. "Hansen's Law" pointed to an anticipated decline of ethnicity in the second generation and a resurgence in the third, with the group gradually thinning out in the fourth and succeeding generations. Empirical observations by Patti and Herrmann (1981) in Bloomfield, an Italian working class neighbor-

[1] Israel Zangwill, *The Melting Pot.* (New York: Macmillan, 1909).

[2] Stokely Carmichael, and Charles H. Hamilton, *Black Power: The Politics of Liberation in America.* (New York: Random House, 1967).

[3] Horace M. Kallen, *Culture and Democracy in the United States.* (New York: Boni and Liveright, 1924).

SAN ANTONIO MAYOR Charles K. Quin holding the flag of the Christopher Columbus Italian Society. Guilio Meloni is shown with Quin. San Antonio, Texas ca. 1930.
— *Courtesy The San Antonio Light Collection,*
The University of Texas Institute of Texan Cultures,
at San Antonio, Texas

MEMBERS OF the San Antonio Missions baseball team and an umpire eating spaghetti lunch. (L. to R.): Emil Bildilli, Art Passarella (umpire), Tony Criscola, and Johnny Lucadillo. San Antonio, Texas. Published 2 June 1939.

— Courtesy The San Antonio Light Collection,
The University of Texas Institute of Texan Cultures
at San Antonio

hood within the city of Pittsburgh, Pennsylvania, "indicates Hansen's Law is at work" there. "Youthful boosterism in Bloomfield coincides with the emergence of the third generation, the grandchildren about whom Hansen wrote." [4] Another theory suggests that ethnic differences tend to disappear in the third generation in the "triple melting pot," resulting in religiously identified Catholics, Protestants, and Jews who have lost their national identifications.[5] Some writers perceive a more or less straight line of cultural and social assimilation, with ethnic consciousness diminishing in each succeeding generation. Other writers identify another aspect of the situation by pointing out the relatedness of ethnic values and social class factors.[6] Milton M. Gordon amplifies this by suggesting that people of the same social class tend to act alike and have the same social values, adding that they often confine their primary group social participation to the "ethclass," the social class segment within their own ethnic group.[7] It appears that people of the same social class tend to think and behave similarly even when they have different ethnic backgrounds. Consequently, social class groupings may also become interethnic, especially where opportunities for in-group association are more limited.

Rudolph L. Biesele (1930) and Terry G. Jordan (1966) have conducted studies of German rural settlements in Texas during the nineteenth century, and T. Lindsay Baker (1979) has researched the first Polish resi-

[4] Marcus L. Hansen, "The Third Generation in America," *Commentary*. Vol. 14, no. 5, November, 1952; William Simons, Samuel Patti, and George Herrmann, "Bloomfield: An Italian Working Class Neighborhood," *italian americana*, Vol. 7, no. 1, Fall/Winter 1981, pp. 112-113.

[5] Will Herberg, *Protestant-Catholic-Jew*. (Garden City, N.Y.: Anchor Books, 1960).

[6] Herbert J. Gans, *The Urban Villagers*. (New York: The Free Press, 1962).

[7] Milton M. Gordon, *Assimilation in American Life*. (New York: Oxford University Press, 1964).

CAVALIERE MICHELE RIZZO (right), President Emeritus, Christopher Columbus Italian Society of San Antonio, is presented a recognition award for outstanding community service by Mr. Vic Pisano (left), former president of the organization.

THE SPIRIT of Italy in Texas is kept alive today by Italian organizations in the state. Mr. Emilio Biondi (right), President of the Italian Club of Dallas, offered an assortment of delicious Italian foods at the Columbus Day Festival, October 12, 1982, Dallas, Texas.

JOSEPH A. DEVANY (Giuseppe A. di Giovanni). Republican Nominee for Congressman from the 5th Congressional District in the November 1982 elections. He states that: "Texas is blessed with the arrival of Italians who introduced a magnificent culture to our state."

dents in the state. Biesele wrote a monumental book, titled *The History of the German Settlements in Texas, 1831-1861,* in which he documented the contributions of German settlers to the political, economic, and social life of Texas.[8] The book is an excellent general source on the early German rural communities in the state. Jordan reveals the importance of cultural heritage in the agricultural systems of immigrant groups. The partial assimilation of the German farmers in Texas was facilitated by emigrant guidebooks, and by direct contact with the southern Anglo-American population of Texas. Assimilation was also facilitated through an apprenticeship period in which many newly arrived immigrants worked for several years on the farms of other Germans who had arrived previously and were already partially assimilated

[8] Rudolph L. Biesele, *The History of the German Settlements in Texas: 1831-1861.* (Austin: Press of Von Boeckmann-Jones, 1930).

agriculturally, and by the numerous agricultural societies founded by Germans in Texas.

However, Jordan also points out that the Germans were an alien group to Texas, whose agricultural heritage was greatly different from that of the native southerners in the state, and, as a result, those important farming traits which survived tended to differentiate them from the Americans. Examples include the greater intensity, productivity, and locational stability of the German farmers, as well as their high rate of land ownership. Jordan concludes that ". . . the German-American farmers of Texas still retain a measure of distinctiveness today." [9] Baker gives a detailed account of the founding and history of the oldest Polish communities in the United States. Established in south-central Texas in the 1850s by immigrants from the region of Upper Silesia, to this day, those settlements continue to retain elements of their regional folk culture, much of which has since disappeared in Europe. [10]

John P. Roche (1982) investigated ethnic attitudes among Italian Americans from two suburbs of Providence, Rhode Island. Examining attitudinal ethnicity and ethnic behavior by suburb, occupational status, and generation, Roche came to some interesting conclusions. According to his study, the dominant pattern within both communities is declining ethnic attachments with each succeeding generation. [11] The findings support those who stress the homogenizing influences present in American society. The forces of education, suburbanization, upward mobility, and succeeding generation tend to make for a decline in ethnicity. The results of the studies conducted

[9] Terry G. Jordan, *German Seed in Texas Soil: Immigrant Farmers in Nineteenth-Century Texas.* (Austin: University of Texas Press, 1966), p. 202.

[10] T. Lindsey Baker, *The First Polish Americans: Silesian Settlements in Texas.* (College Station: Texas A&M Press, 1979).

[11] John P. Roche, "Suburban Ethnicity: Ethnic Attitudes and Behavior Among Italian Americans in Two Suburban Communities," *Social Science Quarterly.* Vol. 63, no. 1, March, 1982, p. 152.

by Roche uphold assimilationist theory and fail to support those who propose a recent rise in ethnicity or a return to the ethnic group in the third generation. "Hansen's Law" does not seem to apply to Italian Americans living in the suburbs of Providence.

However, in both suburbs sixty percent or more of the respondents in each generation and status group reported that at least half of the their friends are of Italian background. In the ethnic suburb among blue-collar workers there was a steady decline for each succeeding generation, while among white-collar workers there was a slight increase reported in the third generation.[12] Roche's study demonstrates that approximately one out of four of the people surveyed shop at an Italian store frequently.[13] If it is assumed that the person purchasing the groceries is obtaining them for his or her family, then it can be further assumed that Italian food is often served in the homes of the respondents. The findings of Roche imply that ethnicity in both its attitudinal and behavioral aspects is considerably lower among those groups which represent likely future trends. However, Rhode Island's large Italian American population may serve to inhibit the kind of ethnic consciousness that comes into being when a group is a small minority, as is the case of Italian Texans.

Despite the important works of Biesele, Jordan, Baker, Roche, and others, until now there have been no serious studies of the early Italian settlements in Texas. Between May 8, 1980, and April 15, 1982, the author conducted research on Italian ethnicity in Texas. The initial funding for this program was provided by a grant from the Texas Committee for the Humanities.[14] The re-

---

[12] *Ibid.*, p. 151.

[13] *Ibid.*, p. 150.

[14] Grant No. M80-710-PG — During interviews, four different types of measurements suggested by Cook and Selltiz (1975) were used as a basis for determining attitudes about Italian ethnicity. See Stuart Cook and Claire Selltiz, "A Multiple-indicator Approach to Measurement," in *Attitude Measurement*. Ed. Gene Summers, Rand McNally & Company, Chicago, 1975, pp. 25-26.

HUMBERTO and CARLO TIRONE. These fourth generation Italian Texans demonstrate pride in their Italian heritage.

sults of this research indicate that today's Italian Texan bears little resemblance to his forebears. Many of the cultural characteristics that once distinguished him have disappeared. Except for members of the older generation, the Italian language has fallen into disuse. In order to survive and prosper, Italian Texans gradually adapted to the dominant culture surrounding them. Eventually, they assimilated many of the values of the southern Anglo-American group. Intermarriage took place, and the Italians by degrees adopted local customs, attitudes, and skills. Today, preference for an Italian spouse and friends has become the exception rather than the rule. Assimilation was inevitable. With so few of their countrymen in the state, the Italians were required to form increasing numbers of friendships and associations with people outside of their own ethnic group.

Hence, the Italian experience in Texas largely supports the theory of assimilation. That is, their experience offers an example of the transformation of immigrant culture: a manifold and ongoing process. While Italians discarded some aspects of their Old World culture in the adjustment to the new society, they retained other aspects. But very little of their heritage was left untouched. The experience of migration and resettlement encouraged the newcomers to regenerate their culture through the development of novel forms, which, in some cases, had little similarity to traditional forms. With regard to theories about the predicted decline or resurgence of ethnicity, research on the Italians in Texas is compatible with "Hansen's Law." That is, first and second generation Italian Texans were largely committed to assimilation, but third generation Americans living in the state demonstrate considerable interest in their ethnic identity. These people appear to feel very secure about their American citizenship, and this allows them the luxury of exploring their Italian roots. Children of marriages in which only one parent is of Italian lineage often inculcate an ethnic identity, whenever they retain the Italian surname, or live with a relative or guardian who was born in Italy. Statistics obtained from interviewing hundreds of third generation Italian Texans in Bryan, San Antonio, Montague, Dallas, Houston, Victoria, Dickinson, and Mingus, as a result of the grant from the Texas Committee for the Humanities, demonstrate that many of these people define themselves, and are defined by others, as possessing certain distinguishing cultural attributes, some of which are shared by other ethnic groups. Although there are exceptions, and individual attitudes are often ambivalent and self-contradictory, these attributes include:

(1) Membership in the Roman Catholic Church.

(2) Pride in the achievements of Italy in the fields of music and art.

(3) Knowledge of Italian terms and phrases.

(4) Knowledge of customs pertaining to the preparation, cooking, and eating of Italian cuisine. The social context in which Italian food is eaten by Italian Americans is very important. Most commonly, it is prepared for family members and close friends. If both the husband and wife are of Italian descent, the meal is ordinarily planned and cooked by the woman, with or without the help of her daughters. When the husband is of Italian lineage but the wife is not, the man usually prepares the meal. These dinners are ordinarily served on Sunday afternoons, but also on Friday and Saturday evenings. The average woman is capable of preparing several Italian dishes, whereas most men concentrate on only a few specialties.

(5) Familiarity with Italian games, folk music, dances, and other forms of entertainment.

(6) A preference for Italian folk music over all other kinds of folk music.

But taped interviews with scores of Italian Texans indicate that an "Italian consciousness" does not depend upon any of these factors. Rather, they merely facilitate the formation or maintenance of an ethnic identity. What is essential, is a group perception of having accomplished important things in the past, and the desire to accomplish them in the future. Ethnic identity depends upon common values and sympathies. Many Italian Americans appear to share an unconscious constellation of feelings, thoughts, perceptions, and memories, based upon similar experiences in childhood, which give rise to common ideas and images. Among some members of this ethnic group there is frequently an immediate, subliminal understanding, based upon shared values and attitudes, which is conveyed through body gestures and facial expressions. Ethnic identification exists when people share a common outlook and agree that they are a distinct group who ought to associate with one another and form organizations with social, cultural, and political goals.

The findings of Jordan and Baker regarding German and Polish settlements in Texas, also apply to Italian rural communities in Texas. Like Baker's Poles, Italians have retained elements of their regional folk culture. Italian farmers are similar to Jordan's Germans in their intensity, productivity, and locational stability, and they have maintained a high rate of land ownership. Italians are still coming to Texas. The immigrants who have arrived since World War II are mainly trained professionals, or skilled workers who are easily assimilated into the fabric of American life. No matter when they came, most Italian Texans are proud of their ancestry. They are also proud of their contributions toward making Texas a better place in which to live.

APPENDICES

POLITICAL EVENTS IN ITALY DURING THE PERIOD OF GREATEST MIGRATION TO TEXAS

The Roman Question, that is, the settlement of relations between the Italian state and the Catholic church after the seizure of Rome in 1870, remained the most vexatious and seemingly insoluble problem confronting Italian governments for almost sixty years. Pope Pius IX refused to consider Camillo di Cavour's proposal in 1860 for "a free church in a free state," which was intended to guarantee the ecclesiastical freedom of the Italian church, uninhibited by government intervention, in return for the renunciation of the pope's temporal claims to Rome. Pope Pius IX noted that Cavour's words contrasted markedly with his record of anticlerical legislation in Piedmont but, more important, he adamantly stood by the position that papal sovereignty in Rome was essential for carrying out the spiritual mission of the church.

Agitation mounted — especially from Giuseppe Mazzini's republicans looking to discredit the Savoy monarchy — for armed intervention in Rome. When the French garrison was withdrawn in 1870, Italian troops occupied the city. A plebiscite confirmed its annexation, and the next year the Italian capital was transferred to Rome. Still hoping for an equitable accommodation with the papacy, Parliament enacted the Law of Guarantees in 1871, which would establish the Vatican as an independent papal territory within the city of Rome and accord the pope the dignity of a sovereign. Pius IX rejected the offer, to the disappointment of many Catholics, and proclaimed himself the "prisoner of the Vatican." As far as the Italian government was concerned, the law stood in force awaiting the pope's agreement. For his part Pius IX refused to recognize the legality of the Italian state, excommunicated King Victor Emmanuel II, and condemned the occupation of Rome as an aggressive act, appealing to foreign powers to restore the city to the papacy. In retaliation the Italian government sharply restricted the civil rights of the clergy.

The impasse between the pope and the state created a crisis of conscience for Italian Catholics who wanted to reconcile their intense devotion to the church with their natural love for their country, their dilemma made even more difficult by the pope's prohibition of Catholics voting in national elections or participating in national politics as being inexpedient. Rather than challenge the anticlericalism of the liberals on their own ground — in Parliament — the church chose instead to organize the Catholic masses socially and economically outside the political system through church-sponsored unions and cooperatives. The government was thereby virtually left to the anticlericals; potential Catholic leadership was cut off from the political life of the nation.

The Italian Parliament was composed of the appointed Senate and the Chamber of Deputies, elected by a restricted electorate. Early governments were dominated by Piedmontese politicians. The party structure was loose and undisciplined. The right, based on Cavour's liberal coalition, stood for national stability and drawing the parts of the country closer together through a highly centralized state administration. The left, composed of ex-republicans and Mazzini's followers, advocated social reform and a more democratic electorate. With the passing of Cavour's political generation in the 1870s, the quality of leadership in Parliament appeared to diminish. After 1876 the left continually maintained a parliamentary majority, but so many factions within it — usually brought together by a single personality — vied for recognition that clearly defined party government, necessary for rigorous parliamentary life, was impossible.

What the Italians substituted for party government was *trasformismo* (flexible and adaptable to changes). Seats in the cabinet were allocated to factional or regional leaders, and as a result governments were formed whose members were so divided in outlook that coherent programs could seldom be formulated and, with all good intentions on the part of the government, reform measures were difficult to realize. Only the Italian Socialist Party, organized in 1892, offered a precise program of social and political reform, and by 1900 it controlled twenty-five percent of the seats in the Chamber of Deputies. However, the strength of the party was diminished by ideological divisions within the party. The spectacular growth of socialism prompted a rapprochement between the ruling Liberals under the reformist prime minister Giovanni Giolitti and the Catholics in 1904. Giolitti's government introduced universal male suffrage in 1912, raising the number of eligible voters from 3.3 to 8.6 million.

Italy, an economically underdeveloped country, was late in entering Europe's scramble for overseas possessions, but Prime Minister Francesco Crispi pursued a determined expansionist policy in the 1880s and 1890s to ensure Italy's place among the European colonial powers. Crispi was not contented with the two strips of land — in Eritrea and Somalia — on the horn of Africa, acquired in 1889; but an attempt to penetrate Ethiopia in 1896 failed at the battle of Adowa. Expansionism remained an aspect of Italy's foreign policy, and the kingdom's colonial holdings increased with the occupation of Libya and the Dodecanese during the war with Turkey (1911-12). The Italians also established spheres of interest in the Balkans and Asia Minor through the construction of port facilities and railroads and the exploitation of resources. Throughout the early colonial experience Italy's interests were concerned primarily with economic rather than political expansion.

Italy adhered to the Triple Alliance with Germany and Austria in 1882, but after 1900 Italian foreign policy tended toward closer ties with France and Great Britain. At the outbreak of World War I in 1914 Italy declared its neutrality, explaining that under the Triple Alliance its commitments were solely defensive in nature. Whereas the Giolitti government opposed entry into the war, public opinion, urged on by the popular press, democratic sentiment, and irredentists who saw the war as an opportunity to complete the *Risorgimento* (the movement for political unity), prevailed. Under the terms of the secret London Pact Italy was promised the Italian-speaking areas held by Austria as well as colonial concessions. Accordingly in May 1915 Italy declared war on Austria. Psychologically Italy was conditioned for war, but the Italian armed forces were unprepared.

By the end of the war Italy had mobilized five million men, and more than 600,000 had been killed. But Italy's case was not well presented at the Versailles Conference and its bargaining position was compromised by unstable conditions at home. Under the terms of the Treaty of St. Germain in 1919, Austria surrendered Istria, Zara in Dalmatia, Trentino-Alto Adige (South Tyrol), and — of strategic importance — control of the Brenner Pass. However, the extravagant offers made in the London Pact were held to be contrary to the spirit of President Woodrow Wilson's Fourteen Points, and the United States refused to support further Italian territorial claims. In 1922 Benito Mussolini came to power and, in the course of the next few years, eliminated the old political parties, curtailed personal liberties, and installed a Fascist dictatorship called the Fascist State. The king, with little or no power, remained titular head of state.

POLITICAL EVENTS IN TEXAS DURING THE
PERIOD OF GREATEST ITALIAN IMMIGRATION

Richard B. Hubbard served as governor of Texas from December 1, 1876 to January 21, 1879. During his administration he strengthened the border defenses of the state, reorganized the penal system, further reduced the state debt, and worked to suppress land frauds. His successor, Oran M. Roberts, inaugurated a pay-as-you-go policy in an attempt to end a state government deficit. His two terms were also distinguished for educational legislation. An Act provided for the University of Texas in compliance with constitutional mandate, and the Sam Houston and Prairie View schools for white and Negro students, respectively, were also established. The Texas educational system continued to improve, and the University of Texas at Austin opened in 1883.

Fence cutting in West Texas posed a serious problem. Barbed wire was first used in Texas about 1879 and its use spread throughout the range by 1883. Conflict arose between cattlemen who continued to depend on the open range and people who were buying and fencing land; also between the big rancher and the small farmer who sometimes found his holdings fenced within a big ranch. Encounters also occurred between the big ranchers. A special session of the Texas State Legislature passed a law which made fence cutting a felony but required that gates be placed every three miles and made it a felony to fence unowned lands. The new law ended the problem. With the fencing of the range, cattle breeding and ranch improvements became more profitable, as the search for underground water increased, and windmills came into greater usage.

James S. Hogg was elected governor of Texas in 1891. Under his administration the Railroad Commission of Texas was established and the legislature passed the Alien Land Law which forbade the ownership of land by aliens, with certain exceptions. Trusts also presented a problem in Texas. Between 1887 and 1899 the Texas State Legislature passed a number of laws opposed to trusts, or combinations designed to control or centralize industries. During the Spanish-American War, Texas sent about 10,000 soldiers to the front. The famous Rough Riders, commanded by Colonel Leonard Wood and Lieutenant Colonel Theodore Roosevelt, were organized at San Antonio.

At the turn of the century, about three million people lived in Texas. More than 82.9 percent of them lived in rural areas, as agriculture strongly dominated the economy. Except for the rich coal mines at Thurber, neither minerals nor manufacturing had become significant. But great changes soon occurred. In 1901 the Spindletop well was the first important oil discovery in the state. This was the beginning of many huge oil fields and of related industries. Two large meat-packing plants were built in the same year at Fort Worth, launching full-scale processing of one of the state's principal raw materials. Other agricultural processing industries developed rapidly. The administration of Governor S. W. T. Lanham, which began in 1903, was distinguished by the adoption of the Terrell Election Law and the inauguration of the popular primary. This law did away with the convention system of nominating candidates for political parties having more than a minimal support.

Governor O. B. Colquitt took office on January 17, 1911. Colquitt's administration was notable for economy in state affairs, reform in the penal system, steps to protect the border along the Rio Grande, which was menaced by revolution and lack of stable government in Mexico, and by passage of the first eight-hour labor law. Other important laws passed during this period include the first law regulating the number of hours of women laborers, a child labor law, a workmen's compensation act, home rule for cities of more than 5,000 residents and judicial reforms. Almost from the entry of the United States in World War I, in April 1917, Texas played a leading role in training men for military service. Italians and Texans fought and died for a similar cause, as more than 200,000 Texans saw service during that war. Under the administration of Governor William P. Hobby, which began in 1917, the compulsory school attendance law was strengthened, free textbooks for public schools were provided, aid for rural schools was increased, and the general scholastic apportionment was raised. An Act of the Texas State Legislature granted women the right to vote in 1918.

During 1917 and 1918 middle West Texas suffered terrible drouths. In an effort to relieve the problem the legislature passed several measures. Governor Hobby was instrumental in obtaining loans for the farmers. Texas became dry in another way when the legislature ratified the national prohibition amendment on February 28, 1918. Pat M. Neff became governor of Texas in 1921. Neff's administration was notable for its educational and prison surveys, and the creation of a prison advisory welfare commission. He originated the state parks movement and appointed the first State Parks Board after it was established by the legislature. He also issued the first official program for a Texas State Centennial which was held in 1936. Neff also declared martial law to suppress crime and to handle a railroad strike situation, and reversed the former liberal pardon policy.

IMMIGRATION RESTRICTION
The Laws of 1917 and 1921

(U.S. Bureau of Immigration, *Annual Report of the Commissioner-General of Immigration, 1923,* p. 2 ff.)

The law of 1917, passed over the veto of President Wilson, marked a definite end to our traditional Immigration policy: the act of 1921 with its quota system inaugurated the present policy of severe restriction. This summary of the two important laws is given in lieu of the acts themselves. For a collection of Documents on Immigration, see E. Abbott, *Selected Documents on Immigration; Historical Aspects of the Immigration Problem.* A brief history of the legislation of the nineteen-twenties can be found in C. P. Howland, ed. *Survey of American Foreign Relations: 1929.*

Perhaps it is not very generally realized that the per centum limit law marked the beginning of actual restriction or limitation of immigration to the United States from Europe, Africa, Australia, and a considerable part of Asia. The Chinese exclusion act of 1882, the passport agreement with Japan which became effective in 1908, and the "barred zone" provision in the general immigration law of 1917 had already stopped or greatly reduced the influx of oriental peoples, but so far as others, and particularly Europeans, were concerned, all applicants who met the various tests prescribed in the general law were admitted. This general law, first enacted in 1882 and several times revised and strengthened, was and still is based on the principle of selection rather than of numerical restriction. It is probably true that the provision barring illiterate aliens from admission, which was added to the general law in 1917, was intended as a restrictive measure rather than a quality test, but in its practical effect it was only another addition to the already numerous class of alleged undesirables who were denied admission, and obviously could not be relied upon actually to limit the volume of immigration.

The immigration act of 1882, which, as already indicated, was the first general law upon the subject, provided for the exclusion from the United States of the following classes only: Convicts, lunatics, idiots, and persons likely to become a public charge. This law underwent more or less important revisions in 1891, 1893, 1903, 1907, and 1917, until the last-mentioned act, which is the present general immigration law, denies admission to many classes of aliens, including the following: Idiots, imbeciles, feeble-minded persons, epileptics, insane persons; persons who have had one or more attacks of insanity at any time previously; persons of constitutional psychopathic inferiority; persons with chronic alcoholism; paupers; professional beggars; vagrants; persons afflicted with tuberculosis in any form or with a loathsome or dangerous contagious disease; persons certified by the examining physician as being mentally or physically defective, such physical defect being of a nature which may affect the ability of the alien to earn a living; persons who have been convicted of or admit having committed a felony or other crime or misdemeanor involving moral turpitude; polygamists, or persons who practice polygamy or believe in or advocate the practice of polygamy; anarchists and similar classes; immoral persons and persons coming for an immoral purpose; contract laborers; persons likely to become a public charge; persons seeking admission within one year of date of previous debarment or deportation; persons whose ticket or passage is paid for with the money of another or who are assisted by others to come, unless it is affirmatively shown that such persons do not belong to one of the foregoing excluded classes; persons whose ticket or passage is paid for by any corporation, association, society, municipality, or foreign government, either directly or indirectly; stowaways; children under 16 years of age unless accompanied by one or both of their parents; persons who are natives of certain geographically defined territory; aliens over 16 years of age who are unable to read some language or dialect; certain accompanying aliens, as described in the last proviso of section 18 of the act; and persons who have arrived in Canada or Mexico by certain steamship lines. Persons who fail to meet certain passport requirements were added to the excluded classes in subsequent legislation.

Obviously it would be difficult to find, or even to invent, many other terms denoting individual undesirability which might be added to the foregoing list, but, as already pointed out, the general law is essentially selective in theory, for even its most rigid application with respect to the excludable classes above enumerated could not be depended upon to prevent the coming of unlimited numbers of aliens who were able to meet the tests imposed.

Even a casual survey of congressional discussions of the immigration problem during the past quarter of a century demonstrates very clearly that while the law makers were deeply concerned with the mental, moral, and physical quality of immigrants, there developed as time went on an even greater concern as to the fundamental racial character of the constantly increasing numbers who came. The record of alien arrivals year by year had shown a gradual falling off in the immigration of northwest European peoples, representing racial stocks which were common to America even in colonial days, and a rapid and remarkably large increase in the movement from southern and eastern European countries and Asiatic Turkey. Immigration from the last-named sources reached an annual average of about 750,000 and in some years nearly a million came, and there seems to have been a general belief in Congress that it would increase rather than diminish. At the same time no one seems to have anticipated a revival of the formerly large influx from the "old sources," as the countries of northwest Europe came to be known.

This remarkable change in the sources and racial character of our immigrants led to an almost continuous agitation of the immigration problem both in and out of Congress, and there was a steadily growing demand for restriction, particularly of the newer movement from the south and east of Europe. During the greater part of this period of agitation the so-called literacy test for aliens was the favorite weapon of the restrictionists, and its widespread popularity appears to have been based quite largely on a belief, or at least a hope, that it would reduce to some extent the stream of "new" immigration, about one-third of which was illiterate, without seriously interfering with the coming of the older type, among whom illiteracy was at a minimum.

Presidents Cleveland and Taft vetoed immigration bills because they contained a literacy test provision, and President Wilson vetoed two bills largely for the same reason. In 1917, however, Congress passed a general immigration bill which included the literacy provision over the President's veto, and, with certain exceptions, aliens who are unable to read are no longer admitted to the United States. At that time, however, the World War had already had the effect of reducing immigration from Europe to a low level, and our own entry into the conflict a few days before the law in question went into effect practically stopped it altogether. Consequently, the value of the literacy provision as a means of restricting European immigration was never fairly tested under normal conditions.

The Congress, however, seemingly realized that even the comprehensive immigration law of 1917, including the literacy test, would afford only a frail barrier against the promised rush from the war-stricken countries of Europe, and in December, 1920, the House of Representatives, with little opposition, passed a bill to suspend practically all immigration for the time being. The per centum limit plan was substituted by the Senate, however, and the substitute prevailed in Congress, but it failed to become a law at the time because President Wilson withheld executive approval. Nevertheless, favorable action was not long delayed, for at the special session called at the beginning of the present administration the measure was quickly enacted, and, with President Harding's approval, became a law on May 19, 1921. This law expired by limitation June 30, 1922, but by the act of May 11, 1922, its life was extended to June 30, 1924, and some strengthening amendments were added.

The principal provisions of the per centum limit act, or the "quota law," as it is popularly known, are as follows:

The number of aliens of any nationality who may be admitted to the United States in any fiscal year shall not exceed 3 percent of the number of persons of such nationality who were resident in the United States according to the census of 1910.

Monthly quotas are limited to 20 percent of the annual quota.

For the purposes of the act, "nationality" is determined by country of birth.

The law does not apply to the following classes of aliens: Government officials; aliens in transit; aliens visiting the United States as tourists or temporarily for business or pleasure; aliens from countries immigration from which is regulated in accordance with treaties or agreement relating solely to immigration, otherwise China and Japan; aliens from the so-called Asiatic barred zone; aliens who have resided continuously for at least five years in Canada, Newfoundland, Cuba, Mexico, Central or South America, or adjacent islands; aliens under the age of 18 who are children of citizens of the United States.

Certain other classes of aliens who are counted against quotas are admissible after a quota is exhausted. The following are included in this category: Aliens returning from a temporary visit abroad; aliens who are professional actors, artists, lecturers, singers, ministers of any religious denomination, professors for colleges or seminaries, members of any recognized learned profession, or aliens employed as domestic servants.

So far as possible preference is given to the wives and certain near relatives of citizens of the United States, applicants for citizenship and honorably discharged soldiers, eligible to citizenship, who served in the United States military or naval forces at any time between April 6, 1917, and November 11, 1918.

Transportation companies are liable to a fine of $200 for each alien brought to a United States port in excess of the quota and where such fine is imposed the amount

paid for passage must be returned to the rejected alien.
The quota limit law is in addition to and not in sub-
stitution for the provisions of the immigration laws.

THE IMMIGRATION ACT OF 1924
May 26, 1924

(U.S. Bureau of Immigration, *Annual Report of the
Commissioner-General of Immigration, 1924* p. 24 ff.)

The quotas established by the immigration act of
1921, Doc. No. 422, were unsatisfactory for two reasons:
they admitted too large a number of immigrants; they
did not discriminate sufficiently in favor of immigration
from Northern and Western Europe. The act of 1924
sought to remedy the first defect by reducing the percentage of immigrants admitted in relation to nationals
already in the country from three to two, and remedied
the second by establishing 1890 rather than 1910 as the
basic date. The report and summary of the law of 1924 is
given in lieu of the law itself for purposes of conciseness.
. . . The "Immigration act of 1924". . .
which supplants the so-called quota limit act of May 19,
1921, the latter having expired by limitation at the close
of the fiscal year just ended, makes several very important changes not only in our immigration policy but also
in the administrative machinery of the Immigration Service. Some of the more important changes in these reports will be briefly referred to.

It will be remembered that the quota limit act of
May, 1921, provided that the number of aliens of any nationality admissible to the United States in any fiscal
year should be limited to 3 percent of the number of persons of such nationality who were resident in the United
States according to the census of 1910, it being also provided that not more than 20 percent of any annual quota

could be admitted annually is limited to 2 percent of the population of such nationality resident in the United States according to the census of 1890, and not more than 10 percent of any annual quota may be admitted in any month except in cases where such quota is less than 300 for the entire year.

Under the act of May, 1921, the quota area was limited to Europe, the Near East, Africa, and Australasia. The countries of North and South America, with adjacent islands, and countries immigration from which was otherwise regulated, such as China, Japan, and countries within the Asiatic barred zone, were not within the scope of the quota law. Under the new act, however, immigration from the entire world, with the exception of the Dominion of Canada, Newfoundland, the Republic of Mexico, the Republic of Cuba, the Republic of Haiti, the Dominican Republic, the Canal Zone, and independent countries of Central and South America, is subject to quota limitations. The various quotas established under the new law are shown in the following proclamation of the President, issued on the last day of the present fiscal year:

BY THE PRESIDENT OF THE UNITED STATES
OF AMERICA

A PROCLAMATION

Whereas it is provided in the act of Congress approved May 26, 1924, entitled "An act to limit the immigration of aliens into the United States, and for other purposes" that —

"The annual quota of any nationality shall be two per centum of the number of foreign-born individuals of such nationality resident in continental United States as determined by the United States census of 1890, but the minimum quota of any nationality shall be 100 (Sec. 11(a)). . . .

"The Secretary of State, the Secretary of Commerce, and the Secretary of Labor, jointly, shall, as soon as feasible after the enactment of this act, prepare a statement showing the number of individuals of the various nationalities resident in continental United States as determined by the United States census of 1890, which statement shall be the population basis for the purposes of subdivision (a) of section 11 (sec. 12(b)).

"Such officials shall, jointly, report annually to the President the quota of each nationality under subdivision (a) of section 11, together with the statements, estimates, and revisions provided for in this section. The President shall proclaim and make known the quotas so reported." (Sec. 12(e)).

Now, therefore, I, Calvin Coolidge, President of the United States of America acting under and by virtue of the power in me vested by the aforesaid act of Congress, do hereby proclaim and make known that on and after July 1, 1924, and throughout the fiscal year 1924-1925, the quota of each nationality provided in said Act shall be as follows:

Country or area of birth

	Quota 1924-1925
Afghanistan	100
Albania	100
Andorra	100
Arabian peninsula (1, 2)	100
Armenia	124
Australia, including Papua, Tasmania, and all islands appertaining to Australia (3, 4)	121
Austria	785
Belgium (5)	512
Bhutan	100
Bulgaria	100
Cameroon (proposed British mandate)	100
Cameroon (French mandate)	100
China	100
Czechoslovakia	3,073
Danzig, Free City of	228
Denmark (5, 6)	2,789
Egypt	100
Esthonia	124

Ethiopia (Abyssinia)	100
Finland	170
France (1, 5, 6)	3,954
Germany	51,227
Great Britain and Northern Ireland (1, 3, 5, 6)	34,007
Greece	100
Hungary	473
Iceland	100
India (3)	100
Iraq (Mesopotamia)	100
Irish Free State (3)	28,567
Italy, including Rhodes, Dodekanesia, and Castellorizzo (5)	3,845
Japan	100
Latvia	142
Liberia	100
Liechtenstein	100
Lithuania	344
Luxemburg	100
Monaco	100
Morocco (French and Spanish Zones and Tangier)	100
Muscat (Oman)	100
Nauru (proposed British mandate) (4)	100
Nepal	100
Netherlands (1, 5, 6)	1,648
New Zealand (including appertaining islands (3, 4)	100
Norway (5)	6,453
New Guinea, and other Pacific Islands under proposed Australian mandate (4)	100
Palestine (with Trans-Jordan, proposed British mandate)	100
Persia (1)	100
Poland	5,982
Portugal (1, 5)	503
Ruanda and Urundi (Belgium mandate)	100
Rumania	603
Russia, European and Asiatic (1)	2,248
Samoa, Western (4) (proposed mandate of New Zealand)	100

San Marino	100
Siam	100
South Africa, Union of (3)	100
South West Africa (proposed mandate of Union of South Africa)	100
Spain (5)	131
Sweden	9,561
Switzerland	2,081
Syria and The Lebanon (French mandate)	100
Tanganyika (proposed British mandate)	100
Togoland (proposed British mandate)	100
Togoland (French mandate)	100
Turkey	100
Yap and other Pacific islands (under Japanese mandate) (4)	100
Yugoslavia	671

1. (a) Persons born in the portions of Persia, Russia, or the Arabian peninsula situated within the barred zone, and who are admissible under the immigration laws of the United States as quota immigrants, will be charged to the quotas of these countries; and (b) persons born in the colonies, dependencies, or protectorates, or portions thereof, within the barred zone of France, Great Britain, the ____, and who are admissible under the immigration laws of the United States as quota immigrants, will be charged to the quota of the country to which such colony or dependency belongs or by which it is administered as a protectorate.

2. The quota-area denominated "Arabian peninsula" consists of all territory except Muscat and Aden, situated in the portion of that peninsula and adjacent islands, to the southeast of Iraq, of Palestine with Trans-Jordan, and of Egypt.

3. Quota immigrants born in the British self-governing dominions or in the Empire of India, will be charged to the appropriate quota rather than to that of Great Britain and Northern Ireland. There are no quota restrictions for Canada and Newfoundland. . . .

4. Quota immigrants eligible to citizenship in the United States, born in a colony, dependency, or protec-

torate of any country to which a quota applies will be charged to the quota of that country.

5. In contrast with the law of 1921, the immigration act of 1924 provides that persons born in the colonies or dependencies of European countries situated in Central America, South America, or the islands adjacent to the American continents (except Newfoundland and islands pertaining to Newfoundland, Labrador and Canada), will be charged to the quota of the country to which such colony or dependency belongs.

GENERAL NOTE — The immigration quotas assigned to the various countries and quota-areas should not be regarded as having any political significance whatever, or as involving recognition of new governments, or of new boundaries, or of transfers of territory except as the United States Government has already made such recognition in a formal and official manner....

CALVIN COOLIDGE.

THE TREATY WITH FRANCE
September 25, 1839

From H. P. N. Gammel (comp.), *The Laws of Texas,*
1822-1897 (10 vols.; Austin, 1898), II, 655-662.

France was the first European nation to recognize the independence of Texas. Without waiting for the United States to act on the offer of annexation, President Houston had commissioned J. P. Henderson as agent and minister plenipotentiary to Great Britain and France with instructions to secure recognition of independence and commercial treaties. Henderson went first to London, but, unable to interest the British, proceeded to Paris in April, 1838. Fifteen months later, after the outbreak of war between France and Mexico and the receipt of a favorable report from the French agent in Texas, Foreign Minister Marshall Soult, Duke of Dalmatia, agreed to negotiate. A treaty, signed by the two ministers on September 25, was ratified by the Texas Senate on January 14. The following extracts from the treaty include its most significant provisions.

Treaty of Amity, Navigation and Commerce, between the Republic of Texas and his Majesty the King of the French

ARTICLE 1. There shall be perpetual peace and amity between his Majesty the King of the French, his heirs and successors, on the one part, and the Republic of Texas, on the other part; and between the citizens of the two states, without exception of persons or of places.

ARTICLE 2. The French and Texians shall enjoy, in their persons and property, in the entire extent of their respective territories, the same rights, privileges, and exemptions, which are or may be granted to the most favored nation. They shall have the right of disposing freely of their property by sale, exchange, by deed of gift, will, or in any other manner, without any impediment or difficulty. In like manner, the citizens of each, inheriting property in either of the states, may become heirs, without any hindrance, . . . They shall be exempted from all military service, — from all war contributions, — forced loans, — military requisitions, and in every other case, their personal or real estate shall not be subject to any other charge or impost than that which shall be paid by the citizens of the country themselves.

ARTICLE 3. If it should happen that one of the two contracting parties be at war with any other power whatever, the other power shall prohibit their citizens from taking or holding commissions or letters of marque to cruise against the other, or to molest the commerce or property of her citizens.

ARTICLE 4. The two, contracting parties adopt in their mutual relations, the principle "that the flag covers the goods."

If one of the two parties remains neuter when the other may be at war with a third power, the goods covered by the neutral flag shall also be considered to be neutral, even if they should belong to the enemies of the other contracting party.

It is equally understood, that the neutrality of flag protects also the freedom of persons, and that the individuals belonging to a hostile power, who may be found on board a neutral vessel, shall not be made prisoners, unless they are actually engaged in the service of the enemy. . . .

ARTICLE 5. In case one of the contracting parties should be at war with another power, and her ships at sea should be compelled to exercise the right of search, it is agreed that if they meet a vessel belonging to the other, then neutral, party, they shall send their boat on board said vessel with two persons charged to enter on an examination of the nationality and cargo of said vessel. The commanders shall be responsible for all vexations, acts of violence, which they may either commit or tolerate on such occasion. The search shall not be permitted but on board vessels which navigate without convoy. . . .

ARTICLE 6. In case one of the two countries should be at war with a third power, the citizens of the other country, shall have a right to continue their commerce and their navigation with the same power, with the exception of the towns or ports, before which there shall be established an actual and effective blockade. It is fully understood, that this liberty of commerce and navigation, shall not extend to articles reputed contraband of war, . . .

ARTICLE 8. The two contracting parties shall have the right to appoint consuls, vice-consuls, and consular agents in all the cities or ports open to the foreign commerce: . . .

ARTICLE 9. The respective consuls, vice consuls, consular agents, and their chancellors, shall enjoy in the two countries, the privileges which generally belong to their functions, such as ... shall be granted in their places of residence, to the agents of the same rank of the most favored nation.

ARTICLE 10. The archives, and in general all the papers of the offices of the respective consulates, shall be inviolable; and under no pretext, nor in any case, shall they either be seized or searched by the local authorities, ...

ARTICLE 12. The respective Consuls, Vice-Consuls, and Consular agents, shall be charged exclusively with the internal police of the commercial vessels of their nation; and the local authorities shall not interfere, except in cases of riot or disturbance of a nature calculated to affect the public peace, either on shore or on board other vessels.

ARTICLE 13. The respective Consuls, Vice-Consuls, and Consular agents, shall have the right to arrest all sailors who shall have deserted from vessels of war, or merchant vessels belonging to their respective countries, and may send them on board, or to their own country....

ARTICLE 14. French vessels arriving in or sailing out of the ports of Texas, and Texian vessels on their entry in or leaving the port of France, shall not be subject to other or higher duties, ... than those which are paid, or shall be paid by the vessels of the country itself.

ARTICLE 15. The products of the soil, and of the industry of either of the two countries, imported directly into the ports of the other, the origin of which shall be duly ascertained, shall pay the same duties whether imported in French or Texian vessels. In like manner, the products exported will pay the same duties, and will enjoy the same privileges, allocations and drawbacks, which are or shall be allowed on the exportation of the same articles in the vessels of the country from which they are exported.

ARTICLE 16. The cottons of Texas, without distinction of quality, will pay on their entry into the ports of France, when they shall be imported directly in French or Texian vessels, a uniform duty of twenty francs on one hundred kilogrammes.

All reduction of duties which may hereafter be made in favor of the cottons of the United States, shall be equally applied to those of Texas, . . .

ARTICLE 17. From the day of the exchange of the ratifications of the present treaty, the duties at present levied in Texas on all fabrics and other articles of silk, or of which silk shall be a chief component part, imported directly into Texas, the manufacture of France, in French or Texian vessels, shall be reduced one half. It is clearly understood, that if the Texian government reduce the duties upon similar products of other nations, to a rate inferior to one half of the duties now existing, France cannot be obliged, in any case, to pay higher duties than those paid by the most favored nation. The duties at present levied in Texas on the Wines and Brandies of France, also imported directly in French or Texian vessels, shall be reduced, the first two-fifths, and the second one fifth.

It is understood, that in case the Republic of Texas should hereafter think proper to diminish the present duties on Wines and Brandies, the production of other countries, a corresponding reduction shall be made on the Wines and Brandies of France, . . .

ARTICLE 18. The inhabitants of the French colonies, their property and ships, shall enjoy in Texas, and reciprocally the citizens of Texas, their property and ships shall enjoy in the French colonies, all the advantages which are or shall be granted to the most favored nation.

ARTICLE 19. The stipulations of the present treaty shall be prepetual, with the exception of the articles, the fourteenth, fifteenth, sixteenth, seventeenth, and eighteenth, the duration of which is fixed to eight years, counting from the day of the exchange of the ratifications. . . .

Done at Paris, the twenty-fifth day of September, in the year of our Lord, one thousand eight hundred and thirty-nine.

J. PINCKNEY HENDERSON,
MAL. DUC DE DALMATIE.

ADDITIONAL ARTICLES

ARTICLE 1. As the laws of France require, as conditions of the nationality of a vessel, — that it should have been built in France, — that the owner, the captain, and three-fourths of the crew, shall be citizens of France: and Texas, by reason of the particular circumstances in which she is placed, being unable to comply with the same conditions, the two contracting parties have agreed to consider as Texian vessels, those which shall be bona fide the exclusive and real property of a citizen or citizens of Texas, residents of the country for at least two years, and of which the captain and two-thirds of the crew, shall also be bona fide citizens of Texas.

ARTICLE 2. It is understood, that if the Republic of Texas thinks proper, hereafter, to diminish the duties now in force on silk goods, they will maintain between the silk goods the produce of countries beyond the Cape of Good Hope, and similar goods of other countries, a difference of ten percent, in favor of the latter. . . .

J. PINCKNEY HENDERSON,
MAL. DUC DE DALMATIE.

THE TREATIES WITH GREAT BRITAIN
From H. P. N. Gammel (comp.) *The Laws of Texas,*
1822-1897 (10 vols.; Austin, 1898), II, 880-898.

J. P. Henderson, Texas' first envoy to Britain and France, arrived in London in October, 1837, to seek recognition and commercial treaties, but he found Lord Palmerston, secretary of foreign affairs, unwilling to negotiate for a variety of reasons. He then went to Paris where he signed a treaty with France in September, 1839, and after ascertaining that Palmerston's position was unchanged, sailed for Texas.

James Hamilton, who as a special agent to secure loans for Texas had assisted on the French treaty, was named by President Lamar as Henderson's successor. Since it no longer appeared that Texas would be annexed to the United States, Hamilton found the European diplomats more receptive to Texas advances. Completing a treaty with the Netherlands on September 18, 1840, Hamilton went to London, and in October obtained Palmerston's consent to discuss the Texas question. The negotiations led to three treaties: a treaty of commerce and navigation, containing the ordinary provisions included in commercial treaties; a "Convention," obligating Britain to mediate with Mexico in behalf of Texas; and a treaty for the suppression of the African slave trade.

The first two treaties were ratified by the Texas Senate early in 1841, but Palmerston, unwilling to take any chances on the treaty for the suppression of the African slave trade, insisted on exchanging ratifications of the three at the same time. The Texas Senate finally approved the third treaty on January 22, 1842, and ratifications of the three were exchanged in London on June 28, 1842. The extracts which follow contain the most significant provisions of the second and third treaties.

1. CONVENTION FOR BRITISH MEDIATION WITH MEXICO

November 14, 1840

CONVENTION

Whereas Her Majesty the Queen of the United Kingdom of Great Britain and Ireland, being desirous of putting an end to the hostilities which still continue to be carried on between Mexico and Texas, has offered Her Mediation to the Contending Parties, with a view to bring about a pacification between them; and whereas the Republic of Texas has accepted the mediation so offered; the Republic of Texas and Her Britannic Majesty have determined to settle, by means of a Convention, certain arrangements which will become necessary in the event of such pacification being effected, and have for this purpose . . . agreed upon and concluded the following Articles:

ARTICLE 1. The Republic of Texas agrees that if, by means of the Mediation of Her Britannic Majesty, an unlimited Truce shall be established between Mexico and Texas, within thirty days after this present Convention shall have been communicated to the Mexican Government by her Britannic Majesty's Mission at Mexico; and if, within Six Months from the day on which that communication shall have been so made, Mexico shall have concluded a Treaty of Peace with Texas, then and in such case the Republic of Texas will take upon itself a portion, amounting to One Million Pounds Sterling, of the Capital of the Foreign Debt contracted by the Republic of Mexico before the 1st of January, One thousand Eight Hundred and Thirty-Five.

ARTICLE II. The manner in which the Capital of One Million Pounds sterling of Foreign Debt, mentioned in the preceding Article, shall be transferred from the Republic of Mexico to the Republic of Texas, shall be settled hereafter by special Agreement between the Republic of Texas and the Republic of Mexico, under the Mediation of her Britannic Majesty.

ARTICLE III. The present Convention shall be ratified, and the Ratifications shall be exchanged at London, as soon as possible within the space of Nine Months from this date.

In witness whereof, the respective Plenipotentiaries have signed the same, and have affixed thereto the Seals of their Arms.

Done at London, the Fourteenth day of November, in the Year of our Lord One Thousand Eight Hundred and Forty.

J. HAMILTON.
PALMERSTON.

2. TREATY BETWEEN THE REPUBLIC OF TEXAS AND GREAT BRITAIN FOR THE SUPPRESSION OF AFRICAN SLAVE TRADE

November 16, 1840

Her Majesty, the Queen of the United Kingdom of Great Britain and Ireland, wishing to give fuller effect to the principles which form the basis of the Treaties which have been concluded between Great Britain and several other European powers, for the suppression of the African Slave Trade, and the Republic of Texas being likewise desirous of rendering effectual the fundamental article in her Constitution, which declares the said trade piracy, have determined to negotiate and conclude a Treaty for the more effectual extinction of this traffic....

ARTICLE I. The Republic of Texas and Her Majesty, the Queen of the United Kingdom of Great Britain and Ireland, engage to prohibit African Slave Trade, either by their respective citizens or subjects, or under their respective flags, or by means of capital belonging to their respective citizens or subjects, and to declare such trade piracy. And the high contracting parties further declare, that any vessel attempting to carry on the slave trade shall, by that act alone, lose all right to claim the protection of their flag.

ARTICLE II. In order more completely to accomplish the object of the present treaty, the high contracting parties mutually consent that those ships of their respective navies which shall be provided with special warrants and orders, according to the form in Annex A, to this treaty, may visit such merchant vessels of either of the high contracting parties as may upon reasonable grounds, be suspected of being engaged in the aforesaid traffic in slaves, or of having been fitted out for that purpose, or of having, during the voyage on which they are met with by the said cruisers, being engaged in the aforesaid traffic; and that such cruisers may detain, and send or carry away such vessels, in order that they may be brought to trial in the manner hereinafter agreed upon.

But the above mentioned right of searching merchant vessels of either of the high contracting parties, shall be exercised only by ships of war, . . . and the said right shall not be exercised within the Mediterranean sea, nor within those seas in Europe which lie without the Straits of Gibralter, and to the northward of the 37th parallel of north latitude, and within and to the eastward of the meridian of longitude, twenty degrees west of Greenwich; nor in the Gulf of Mexico, to the northward of the 25th parallel of north latitude, nor to the westward of the 90th degree of longitude, west of Greenwich.

ARTICLE III. Each of the high contracting parties reserves to itself the right to fix, according to its own convenience, the number of ships of its navy which shall be employed on the service mentioned in the second article of this treaty, and the stations on which such ships shall cruise. . . .

ARTICLE V. . . . The cruizers of the high contracting parties shall afford to each other mutual assistance, on all occasions when it may be useful that they should act in concert.

ARTICLE VI. Whenever a merchant vessel, navigating under the flag of either of the contracting parties, shall have been detained by a cruizer of the other, duly authorized to that effect, conformably to the provisions of this treaty, such merchant vessel, as also her master, her crew, her cargo, and the slaves who may be on board of her, shall be carried to such place as shall have been appointed to that end by the contracting parties, respectively; and they shall be delivered over to the authorities appointed for that purpose by the government within whose territory such place shall be, to be proceeded against before the proper tribunals, as hereinafter directed. . . .

ARTICLE VII. If the commander of a cruizer of either of the contracting parties shall have reason to suspect that a merchant vessel, navigating under convoy of, or in company with, a ship of war of the other contracting party, has been engaged in the slave trade or has been fitted out for the said trade, he is to make known his suspicions to the commander of the ship of war, who shall proceed alone to visit the suspected vessel; and if the last mentioned commander shall find that the suspicion is well founded, he shall cause the vessel, together with her master, her crew, and the cargo, and the slaves who may be on board of her, to be taken into a port of her own nation, to be proceeded against before the proper tribunals, as hereinafter directed.

ARTICLE IX. Any merchant vessel of either of the high contracting parties, which shall be visited and detained in pursuance of the provisions of this treaty, shall, unless proof be given to the contrary, be deemed to have been engaged in the African Slave Trade, or to have been fitted out for the purposes of such traffic, if any of the particulars hereinafter specified shall be found in her outfit or equipment, or to have been on board during the voyage on which the vessel was proceeding when captured, videlicet:

First: — Hatches with open gratings, instead of the close hatches which are usual in merchant vessels;

Secondly: — Divisions or bulk-heads in the hold or on deck, in greater number than are necessary for vessels engaged in lawful trade;

Thirdly: — Spare plank fitted for being laid down as a second or slave deck;

Fourthly: — Shackles, bolts, or handcuffs;

Fifthly: — A larger quantity of water in casks or in tanks, than is requisite for the consumption of the crew of the vessel, as a merchant vessel;

Sixthly: — An extraordinary number of water casks, or of other receptacles for holding liquid; unless the master shall produce a certificate from the custom-house at the place from which he cleared outwards, stating that sufficient security had been given by the owners of such vessel, that such extra quantity of casks or of other receptacles should only be used to hold palm-oil, or for other purposes of lawful commerce;

Seventhly: — A greater quantity of mess-tubs or kids, than are requisite for the use of the crew of the vessel, as a merchant vessel.

Eighthly: — A boiler, or other cooking apparatus, of an unusual size, and larger, and fitted for being made larger, than requisite for the use of the crew of the vessel as a merchant vessel; or more than one boiler, or other cooking apparatus of the ordinary size;

Ninthly: — an extraordinary quantity of rice, of the flour of Brazil manioc, or cassada, commonly called farina, of maize, or of Indian corn, or of any other article of food whatever, beyond what might probably be requisite for the use of the crew; such rice, flour, maize, Indian corn, or other articles of food, not being entered in the manifest, as part of the cargo for trade;

Tenthly: — A quantity of mats or matting, greater than is necessary for the use of the vessel as a merchant vessel.

Any one or more of these several things, if proved to have been found on board, or to have been on board during the voyage on which the vessel was proceeding when captured, shall be considered as prima facie evidence of the actual employment of the vessel in the African Slave Trade; and the vessel shall thereupon be condemned and be declared lawful prize, unless clear and incontestible evidence on the part of the master or owners shall establish, to the satisfaction of the court, that such vessel was, at the time of her detention or capture, employed in some legal pursuit; and that such of the several things, above enumerated, as were found on board her at the time of her detention, or which had been put on board her during the voyage on which she was proceeding when captured, were needed for legal purposes on that particular voyage.

ARTICLE X. A vessel detained as before mentioned, together with her master, crew, and cargo, shall be forthwith proceeded against before the proper tribunals of the country to which she belongs, and shall be tried and adjudged by, and according to, the established forms and laws in force in that country; and if, in consequence of such proceedings, the said vessel shall be found to have been employed in the African Slave Trade, or to have been fitted out for the purposes thereof, the vessel and her equipments, and her cargo of merchandize, shall be confiscated; and the master, the crew, and the accomplices shall be dealt with conformably to the laws by which they have been tried.

If the said vessel shall be confiscated, the proceeds arising from her sale shall, within six months from the date of such sale, be paid into the hands of the government of the country to which the captor belongs, to be distributed according to law among the officers and crew of the capturing ship.

ARTICLE XI. If any of the things specified in Article IX of this treaty shall be found on board, or to have been on board, of any merchant vessel, during the voyage, on which the vessel was proceeding when captured, no compensation for losses, damages, or expenses, consequent upon the detention of such vessel, shall, in any case, be granted, either to her master, or to her owner, or to any other person interested in her equipment or lading, even though sentence of condemnation should not be pronounced against her, in consequence of her detention.

ARTICLE XII. In all cases in which a vessel shall, under this treaty, be detained as having been engaged in the African Slave Trade, or as having been fitted out for the purposes thereof, and shall be adjudged and confiscated accordingly, the government whose cruizer detained the vessel, or the government by whose tribunal the vessel may be condemned, may purchase the condemned vessel for the use of its navy, at a price to be fixed by a competent person, . . .

ARTICLE XIII. When a merchant vessel, detained under this treaty, shall, upon adjudication before the proper tribunal, be held not to have been engaged in the African Slave Trade, and not to be fitted up for the purposes thereof, she shall be restored to her lawful owner or owners; and if, in the course of adjudication, it shall be proved that she has been visited and detained illegally, or without sufficient cause of suspicion; or if it shall be proved that the visit and detention have been attended with any abuse, or with vexatious acts, the commander of the cruizer, . . . or the officer who shall have been appointed to bring her in, and under whom (as the case may be) the abuse or vexatious acts shall have been committed, shall be liable to costs and damages to be paid to the master and to the owners of the vessel and cargo. . . .

ARTICLE XIV. If in the visit or detention of a merchant vessel under this treaty, any abuse or vexation shall have been committed, and if the vessel shall not have been delivered over to the jurisdiction of her own nation, the master of the vessel shall make a declaration, on oath, of the abuses or vexations of which he has to complain, and of the costs and damages to which he lays claim; and . . . the Government of the country to which the officer so charged with abuses and vexations shall belong, shall forthwith institute an inquiry into the matter; and if the complaint be proved to be valid, the said government shall cause to be paid to the master or owner, or to any other person interested either in the vessel which has been molested, or in her cargo, the proper amount of costs and damages.

ARTICLE XVI. The high contracting parties agree to ensure the immediate freedom of slaves who shall be found on board vessels detained and condemned in virtue of the stipulations of the present treaty; and, for this purpose, it is agreed that all slaves found on board a Texian vessel detained in the West Indies, shall, if the vessels be condemned by the Texian tribunals, be delivered over by the Texian to the British authorities, to be conveyed, at the expense of the British government, to some one of the British colonies in the West Indies; and in regard to Texian vessels detained on the coast of Brazil, or on the coast of Africa, it is further agreed that, in order that any slave found on board such vessels may not be exposed to the sufferings which would attend a voyage to Texas, such slaves shall . . . be carried or sent, at once, by the commander of the capturing cruizer, to one of the British settlements on the coast of Africa, the vessel herself being sent on to Galveston for adjudication. . . .

J. HAMILTON.
PALMERSTON.

INDEX